Cryptoeconomics

Cryptoeconomics
Igniting a New Era of Blockchain

Jian Gong and Wei Xu

CRC Press
Taylor & Francis Group
Boca Raton London New York

CRC Press is an imprint of the
Taylor & Francis Group, an **informa** business
AN AUERBACH BOOK

CRC Press
Taylor & Francis Group
6000 Broken Sound Parkway NW, Suite 300
Boca Raton, FL 33487-2742

First issued in paperback 2022

© 2020 by Taylor & Francis Group, LLC
CRC Press is an imprint of Taylor & Francis Group, an Informa business

No claim to original U.S. Government works

ISBN 13: 978-1-03-247451-9 (pbk)
ISBN 13: 978-0-367-42993-5 (hbk)
ISBN 13: 978-1-003-03973-0 (ebk)

DOI: 10.1201/9781003039730

This book contains information obtained from authentic and highly regarded sources. Reasonable efforts have been made to publish reliable data and information, but the author and publisher cannot assume responsibility for the validity of all materials or the consequences of their use. The authors and publishers have attempted to trace the copyright holders of all material reproduced in this publication and apologize to copyright holders if permission to publish in this form has not been obtained. If any copyright material has not been acknowledged please write and let us know so we may rectify in any future reprint.

Except as permitted under U.S. Copyright Law, no part of this book may be reprinted, reproduced, transmitted, or utilized in any form by any electronic, mechanical, or other means, now known or hereafter invented, including photocopying, microfilming, and recording, or in any information storage or retrieval system, without written permission from the publishers.

For permission to photocopy or use material electronically from this work, please access www.copyright.com (http://www.copyright.com/) or contact the Copyright Clearance Center, Inc. (CCC), 222 Rosewood Drive, Danvers, MA 01923, 978-750-8400. CCC is a not-for-profit organization that provides licenses and registration for a variety of users. For organizations that have been granted a photocopy license by the CCC, a separate system of payment has been arranged.

Trademark Notice: Product or corporate names may be trademarks or registered trademarks, and are used only for identification and explanation without intent to infringe.

Publisher's Note
The publisher has gone to great lengths to ensure the quality of this reprint but points out that some imperfections in the original copies may be apparent.

**Visit the Taylor & Francis Web site at
http://www.taylorandfrancis.com**

**and the CRC Press Web site at
http://www.crcpress.com**

Contents

Foreword

Why do you need to read this book?

It's been 6 years since I invested in OKCoin in 2014. During this period, OKCoin (OKex) has become one of the largest cryptocurrency exchanges in the world, but I have to say that I only began to understand blockchain when I started Mars Finance at the end of the last year.

A lot of people can't see the opportunities in blockchain at a glance, because the blockchain is sufficiently subversive and complex. It appears to be an upgraded version of the "decentralized Internet" that was 20 years ago, which seems to be just a technological innovation. But in fact, the blockchain has established a new trust system, and thus, it has brought technology, economy, culture, and even humanity into it, and has chained everything, just like an octopus. I believe this is an opportunity far greater than the Internet. This is an opportunity to "flip the table".

It is not enough to understand such a complex and very new thing from a technical perspective. Therefore, in the community of Mars Finance, many people discuss the issue a little deeper; they touch upon the field of monetary and economics, and even philosophy and theology.

Nowadays, terms such as "bitcoin", "blockchain", "smart contract", and "mining" have entered our daily life. However, many people started to pay attention to blockchain technology more because of the recent rapid growth of cryptocurrency market cap, but not because they recognize blockchain as a technology that can bring us a new revolution by subverting the existing systems and practices.

I really like the idea of "cryptoeconomics". I believe that this term, which is unknown to majority of people, will occupy a very important position in the blockchain. The author of this book, Gong Jian, is an early participant in the Bitcoin community. He began to engage in mining in 2011, and he is also a columnist for *Harvard Business Review* and *The Entrepreneur*. The book he wrote is a systematic review of the structure and context of the blockchain-derived economic model. In my opinion, this is China's first book on cryptoeconomics in popular science. It describes cryptoeconomics in connection with the game theory, behavioral economics, and others in simple understandable language.

The blockchain solves the problem of trust through technology. After the mechanism of cryptoeconomics is written as a code, it can restrict the behavior of everyone in the blockchain through a series of rewards and punishments. This is a great innovation mechanism, automagical, and safe, and it has a consensus.

Wang Feng

Founder of Linekong Interactive Group (HK.8267) and Mars Finance, partner of Geekbang Venture Capital Partner

Preface

Perhaps you are now familiar with the term "blockchain". Blockchain technology has subverted our existing perceptions and will bring us a new revolution.

Although cryptoeconomics is not a well-known concept, it plays a very important role in blockchain. Vlad Zamfir, a developer of Ethereum, explained this term as "a formal discipline that studies protocols that governs the production, distribution, and consumption of goods and services in a decentralized digital economy. Cryptoeconomics is a practical science that focuses on the design and characterization of these protocols".

This book sorted out structures of blockchain-derived economic models and their history, and used actual cases to illustrate the inevitable relationships between cryptoeconomics and blockchain.

Blockchain technology solves trust issues. After the mechanism of cryptoeconomics is written as a code, it can restrict everyone's behavior on blockchain through a reward and punishment system that enables automatic mechanism with consensus in an innovative way. The greatest significance of cryptoeconomics lies in guaranteeing safety, stability, activity, and order in a decentralized consensus system. Security and stability are achieved mainly by cryptographical mechanisms. Activity and order are achieved through economic mechanisms.

As this book discusses about the most popular consensus algorithms in current days as well as optimization mechanisms, those who are interested in and wish to explore the blockchain industry may find this book very useful. At the same time, with examples explained in clear and simple terms that are easy to understand, this book also explores economic mechanisms of blockchain such as game theory and behavioral economics.

Jian Gong

Authors

Jian Gong is a data scientist and technology entrepreneur. He used to be a columnist at Harvard Business Review (China), The Entrepreneur, etc. He was previously the Outstanding Winner of ICM.

Wei Xu is the founder of Huixing Blockchain in China and former COO of Xiaogou Money.

Chapter 1

What Is Cryptoeconomics?

What is cryptoeconomics? Vlad Zamfir, a developer of Ethereum, explains this term as "a formal discipline that studies protocols that govern the production, distribution, and consumption of goods and services in a decentralized digital economy. Cryptoeconomics is a practical science that focuses on the design and characterization of these protocols".

If we leave the concept of cryptoeconomics itself and consider the origin of the word, we can see that it derives from two words: cryptography and economics.

1.1 The Basics of Cryptography

Classical cryptography focuses on writing and transmission of information and corresponding deciphering methods. And modern cryptography originates from a large number of related cryptographic theories that emerged at the end of the 20th century, it is a branch of mathematics and computer science, and at the same time, it refers a lot to an information theory. Modern cryptography focuses not only on the confidentiality of information but also on information integrity verification, non-repudiation of information (i.e., digital signatures), and all information security issues, arising from internal and external attacks that emerge in distributed computing.

The development of modern cryptography has promoted the development of computer science, especially the need for computer and network security. Nowadays, cryptography has been applied in daily life, including ATM chips, computer access passwords, e-commerce, and other spheres.

Blockchain technology applies a lot of cryptographic content in its operation, which mainly includes **hash algorithm**, **key encryption**, and **digital signature**.

1.1.1 Hash Algorithm

Hash functions are often referred to as cryptographic hash functions, for example, message digest functions, which do not necessarily use keys, but are associated with many important cryptographic algorithms. It outputs the input data (usually an entire file) into a shorter fixed-length hash value.

This process is one-way, and the possibility of two different inputs producing the same hash value is very low.

Briefly, the hash algorithm maps strings of arbitrary length to shorter, fixed-length strings. For example, Bitcoin (what is the uses the SHA-256 as a digest algorithm, which gives a 256-bit output for any length of input.

So, what are the applications of the hash algorithm in cryptocurrency?

1. Cryptographic hash function

   A cryptographic hash function has the following characteristics:
   - Definiteness: no matter how many times are parsed in the same hash function, if the input is the same, the resulting output is always the same.
   - Efficiency of the calculations: the process of calculating hash values is very efficient.
   - Anti-preimage attack: for a given output, the input is irreversible.
   - The influence of subtle changes: subtle changes in any input can have a dramatic effect on the output of the hash function.

   The cryptographic hash function is very important for the security on blockchain and the mining.

2. Data structure

   In cryptography, there are two kinds of data structures which are important for understanding blockchains: linked list and hash pointer.

   The linked list is a data block that is sequentially connected in order, as shown in Figure 1.1.

   A blockchain is essentially a linked list in which each new block contains a hash pointer. The pointer points to the hash of the previous block and all the data it contains. With it, the blockchain has great features that cannot be changed.

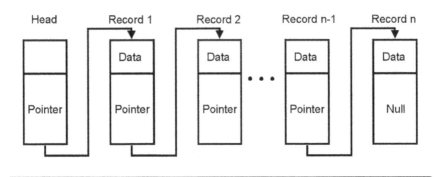

Figure 1.1   Linked List and Hash Pointer Data Structure.

So how does the blockchain achieve immutability?

If someone tries to tamper with the data in the block, let's look at the third feature of the cryptographic hash function: "The effect of subtle changes is that any slight change in the input will have a dramatic impact on the output of the hash function". So, even if someone tries to rewrite the data in the block subtly, it will also cause a huge change in the hash value of Block 1 stored in Block 2, which will cause changes in the hash value of Block 2. The change, in turn, affects the hash value stored in Block 3. No. 3 affects No. 4, No. 4 affects No. 5.… Eventually, the data on the entire blockchain will change. This way of modifying data by freezing the entire chain is almost impossible. Therefore, the blockchain is considered as immutable.

Each block has its own Merkle root. If multiple transactions are included in each block and these transactions are stored linearly, the process of finding a particular transaction in all transactions can become very complicated. That's why we use the Merkel tree.

As it is shown in Figure 1.2, in the Merkel tree, all individual transactions can be traced back to the same root through a hash algorithm, which makes searching very easy. Therefore, if we want to get a specific data in the block, we can search directly through the hash value in the Merkel tree without linear access.

3. Mining

The hash algorithm is very important for mining new encrypted blocks, and its working principle is the adjustment of the difficulty value. A random string named "nonce" is added to the hash of the new block and then hashed again. Next, check if it is lower than the

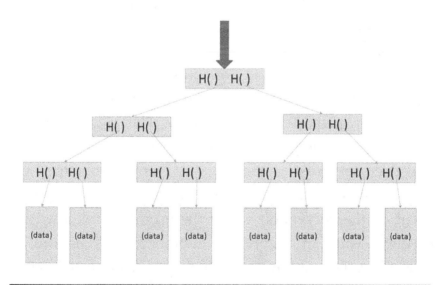

Figure 1.2   Merkel Tree Trace Back Structure.

set difficulty level. If it is lower, the resulting new block will be added to the chain, and the miner responsible for mining will be rewarded. If it is not lower, then the miner continues to modify the random string "nonce" until the value appears below the difficulty level.

1.1.2 *Key Encryption*

Key encryption includes symmetric key encryption and public key encryption.

Symmetric key encryption is an encryption method in cryptography. If you convert one of the numbers, letters, or strings of random letters in the data, the key changes the text or letters in the data in a specific way, such as changing the relative position of the letters (e.g., the word "one" becomes "neo"). As long as the sender and the recipient know the secret key, they can encrypt and decrypt the data and use that data.

Public key encryption, or public key cryptography, also known as asymmetric key cryptography, is another encryption method in cryptography. The biggest feature relative to symmetric key cryptography is that encryption and decryption use different keys. The data obtained by encryption using the encrypted key can only be decrypted by using the decryption key of the user. If you know one of them, you can't figure out another one. Therefore, if one of the keys is disclosed, it does not harm the other one; that is, the publicly opened key is public key, and the undisclosed key is private key.

In symmetric key cryptography, encryption and decryption use the same key, and perhaps different keys are used for different messages, but they all face the challenge of key management. Since each pair of communicating parties must use a different key than the other group, when the number of network members increases, the number of keys increases quadratically. A more complicated problem here is: how do you create a common key for secure communication when there is no secure channel between the two parties? If you have a channel to create a key securely, why not to use an existing channel. This is really a contraction of the matter who came first? It is just a "chicken or egg contradiction".

1.1.3 *Digital Signature*

Digital signatures are the foundation of public key infrastructures (PKIs) and many network security mechanisms (SSL/TLS, virtual private networks, etc.). As it is clear from the name, digital signature is a digitization of ordinary signatures in daily life. The feature of it is that others can easily create signatures, but it is difficult to imitate. Digital signatures can be permanently combined with signed messages and cannot be removed from messages.

A digital signature roughly consists of two algorithms: one is signing using the private key to process the hash value of the message and the other is verification using the public key to verify the authenticity of the signature. Rivest–Shamir–Adleman (RSA) and Digital Signature Algorithm (DSA) are the two most popular digital signature mechanisms.

Let's imagine in real life, why do we sign, what is the role of signatures, and what are their characteristics?

- Verifiability: this signature should prove that it is indeed your handwriting.
- Unforgeability: no one else can forge your signature.
- Non-repudiation: if you sign your document with your own signature, the validity of the file will not be reclaimed, and you can't claim that someone else is signing you instead.

However, in real life, no matter how complicated the signature is, there is a possibility of being forged. Because you can't really verify the validity of a signature with a simple visual aid (such as handwriting identification), it is neither efficient nor reliable.

Cryptography gives us a solution to solve problems through public and private keys. Let's take a look at how these two keys work and how they contribute to the cryptocurrency system.

Let's assume that there are two people, A and B. A wants to send some very important data, and B wants to identify that this data really comes from A; they can achieve this by using A's public and private keys. The public key, as its name suggests, refers to the public key that can be obtained by anyone. The private key is a key owned by the individual and cannot be shared with others. Also, it is not feasible to determine a public key by someone's private key.

Let's return to the topic of A and B sending the data. If they want to use a key to exchange information, how will they do it exactly?

Let's assume that A wants to send the message M. A has a private key K1 and a public key K2. Then, when he sends the message to B, he encrypts the message with the private key, and the message becomes K1(M). When B receives this message, he can use A's public key to get the information, K2K1(M), so that the original information M can be obtained.

The above process is clearly shown in Figure 1.3.

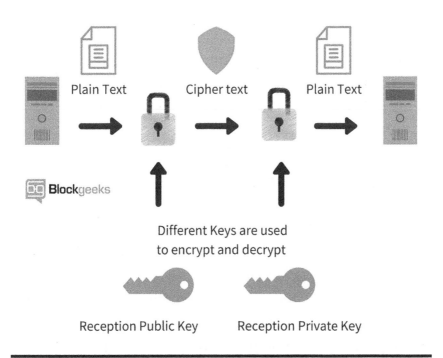

Figure 1.3 **Information Exchange using Public and Private Keys.**

Let us re-examine the features of digital signatures in cryptography through the examples of signatures in everyday life.

- Verifiability: if the encrypted information can be decrypted with Al's public key, it can be approved 100% that A sent the message.
- Unforgeability: if there is another person C, intercepting this message and sending a message of his/her own with its own private key, then A's public key will not be able to decrypt it, because A's public key can only be used to decrypt the information encrypted with its own private key.
- Non-repudiation: similarly, if A claims, "I didn't send the message, it's sent by C", but B can use A's public key to decrypt the information, which proves that A is lying. In this way, A can't recall the information he sent before, and thus can't deny it.

1.2 Basic of Economics

Economics is a complex concept. In this book, we only describe some economic theories that are related to cryptocurrency and blockchain.

The difference between blockchains and other decentralized peer-to-peer systems is that it provides users with financial and economic incentives to complete a job. Like other solid economic systems, we all need people to get the job done through incentives and rewards. Similarly, there are punishments for the miners who act unethically or do not perform their duties.

1.2.1 Incentives

The blockchain uses the following two combinations of incentives:

- **The first type of incentive combination**: Token + Privileges

  Token: cryptocurrency is distributed as a reward to participants who are highly active and contribute to the blockchain.

  Privileges: participants can get the right to make a decision, which gives them the right to collect rent. For example, miners who add new blocks can become temporary decision-makers for creating new blocks, will become dictators of a new block for a short term, and will have the power to decide which transactions have to be added to the block. They can charge a fee for all transactions included in the block.

- **The second type of incentive combination**: Reward + Punishment

  Reward: good participants can get monetary rewards or the right to make decision after fulfilling the work.

  Punishment: bad participants must pay a currency fine or lose their rights because of their malicious behavior.

1.2.2 Punishment

Just like any other effective economic system, there are positive and negative incentives in cryptocurrency. Imagine a matrix of profits shown in Figure 1.4; not only the profit of participants is very high, but the impact on society is also very high.

Let's suppose that there are two people, A and B, who are going to commit crimes. Now, according to the income matrix, when they commit crimes, their returns are high. So they may all choose to commit crimes; although this is logically plausible, it will have a very bad social impact. If everyone in the world is driven by personal greed, the world will become terrible. So, how should human beings deal with the situation in which everyone chooses to do evil? The answer is to introduce a penalty mechanism.

Let's suppose that we have a social system in which, whenever someone commits a crime by taking 0.5 from the system, he/she losses 5 as penalties. So let's add the penalty factor to the income matrix above and then observe the changes in Figure 1.5.

As it is shown in the figure, the benefits have changed dramatically, and not committing crime is the best strategy. Now, the cost of punishment is high, but society has lost

	B doesn't commit crime	B commits crime
A doesn't commit crime	(1,1)	(1,4)
A commits crime	(4,1)	(4,4)

Figure 1.4   Payoff Matrix of a Social System.

	B doesn't commit crime	B commits crime
A doesn't commit crime	(1,1)	(1,-1)
A commits crime	(-1,1)	(-1,-1)

Figure 1.5   Payoff Matrix of a Social System with Penalty Factor.

0.5 for public facilities. This will lead to situations where no one is participating in the social system anymore; what motivates everyone in the community to participate? The answer is that punishment is a coercive measure for everyone, and anyone who does not participate will also be punished. For example, police officers are supported by taxes, so they can punish criminals, but the loss of public facilities will be taken from the public in the form of taxes. Anyone who participates but does not pay taxes will be considered a criminal and punished.

In the blockchain world, any miners who do not follow the rules and mine illegally will be punished, and they will be deprived of their privilege and bear the risk of being socially excluded. Once the proof of equity is adopted, this punishment will become more severe. By using simple game theory and punishment systems, miners can maintain integrity.

1.3 Supply and Demand

Under such incentives and penalties, how can cryptocurrency become valuable? The reason why cryptocurrency and ordinary currency have value is basically the same; that is, based on trust. When people trust a certain commodity and give it value, it becomes a currency. This is why the French currency and gold were valuable at first. Therefore, when a given commodity has a given value, the value changes with the supply and demand relationship, which is the oldest rule in economics.

What are the relationships between supply and demand?

The total amount of Bitcoin is fixed at 21 million. Since the total amount is fixed, there are few things that must be considered when it comes to the supply of Bitcoin. First of all, there are some rules that need to be set to make Bitcoin mining difficult. Otherwise, the miners will be willing to mine, to extract the remaining Bitcoin, and to put it on the market, thus reducing the overall value.

In order to ensure that the miners do not immediately extract all the remaining Bitcoins, we need to use the following means.

First, add a new block to the chain every 10 minutes, and each time you add a block, you can get 25 Bitcoins as a reward. The time interval must be fixed to ensure that the miners do not continue to add blocks on the chain without rules. Second, the Bitcoin protocol requires that the difficulty level will be constantly increasing. As was mentioned earlier, during the mining process, the hash value and the nonce value of the block need to be lower than a certain limit. This value is called the "level of difficulty" and usually starts with a few zeros. If the difficulty increases, the number of zeros also increases. With the above two methods, the mining process has become very professional and got a huge investment. The entire process ensures that all

Bitcoin supply in the market can be verified, which is also applied to other cryptocurrencies based on the proof-of-work mechanism.[1]

Figure 1.6 represents the supply and demand curve, which is the most common chart in economics. As shown in the figure, the demand for goods is inversely related to supply. The intersection of the two curves is the equilibrium point, so let's use this logic to observe the cryptocurrency, such as Bitcoin.

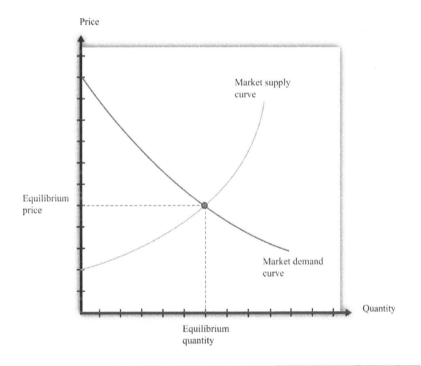

Figure 1.6   Market Supply-Demand Curve.

---

[1] Note: Figures 1.1–1.3 are from https://blockgeeks.com/guides/what-is-cryptoeconomics/, and the original author is Ameer Rosic.

Chapter 2

Mechanisms of Consensus

On February 24, 2018, a speaker from the Bitcoin community, posted an open letter on Twitter calling on the community to revise the consensus mechanism. When this news came out, it caused a sensation. Many Bitcoin enthusiasts spoke sharply, saying that this speaker doesn't understand Bitcoin at all and asked him to abdicate.

Why did this proposal to change the consensus mechanism lead to intense discussions in the whole cryptocommunity? Let us first understand what a consensus mechanism is.

The word "consensus" is presumably familiar to everyone. Different groups can work together, necessarily because they share a common belief. So, in the world of blockchain, what does the term "consensus" mean? Why do we need a consensus?

When you mention blockchain, everyone will think of the "decentralization" feature. In other words, it is de-intermediation. Our current social structure includes various third-party intermediaries such as banks, Taobao, and video websites. For example, Taobao will recommend products according to our shopping habits, letting you be tempted to buy. So can we ask Taobao not to peek into our shopping habits and not to recommend us a shopping list? No. Because Taobao is a centralized organization, and the rules are set by it, which has no need to reach a consensus with us.

But in the world of blockchain, there is no intermediary, which means nobody will set up the rules. Every formulation, change of the rule, etc. needs to reach a common understanding. However, it is hard to please all; everyone sticks to his own views, so it is very difficult to reach a consensus.

Let's use Taobao as an example again. When I buy something, only after I paid the money will the seller ship the goods. If the seller acts like it is never happened, Taobao can simply monitor the records on website and supervise the seller to deliver it to me. Once there is no intermediary agency like Taobao, who will act as a referee? I said that I paid the money and found my friend to testify; the other said that I did not pay, but also found a group of friends to testify. Once this situation happens, it is not clear whether I have ever paid or not.

Therefore, there must be a set of feasible methods to reach a unified opinion. This method is called a consensus mechanism, also known as a consensus algorithm.

2.1 The Byzantine Generals Problem

In 1982, American computer scientist Leslie Lamport raised the problem of Byzantine Generals.

Let's imagine that during the Middle Ages, ten generals of the Byzantine Empire are going to besiege a city. However, the walls of this city, which is strongly fortified, are very high, so only if they attack at the same time, they can success. In other words, ten generals should either attack at the same time or recede at the same time and abandon the attack plan. This requires ten generals to have a discussion together, but they are in different places so they cannot get together. Therefore, there is a minister who must pass the votes of each general, and ten generals will make further decisions based on the results of the voting.

If ten generals are honest and trustworthy, the solution is simple. But there are traitors, so it is more complicated.

Let's assume that four generals are voting for attack, four generals are voting for retreat, and the remaining two are traitors. These two traitors told those generals who want to attack that they will attack, and told those generals who had decided to retreat that they will retreat, which will make it possible to unify the action. Every general must be careful and cannot trust others easily.

So this is the Byzantine Generals Problem: it is about 10 generals who are in different places and constitute a distributed network. Each general is at the same position level, so how can we guarantee common attack or common retreat without any authority and mutual trust?

This problem remains unsolved for 10 years.

In 1999, American computer scientists Miguel Castro and Barbara Liskov proposed a solution, the Practical Byzantine Fault-Tolerant Algorithm (PBFT). The so-called "fault tolerance" allowed bad people to exist in a distributed network. The core calculation formula of the PBFT algorithm is $N \geq 3F + 1$, where N is the total node in the distributed system, and F is the maximum number of problematic nodes. For example, in the case of Byzantine Generals, there are ten generals, $N = 10$, $F = 3$, which means that as long as the number of traitors is less than one-third of the total number, there is a way to reach a consensus.

The specific solutions are following:

1. Oral promotion

   The general can send the people to spread the information about their attack or retreat. The other nine generals receive his news and send people to several other generals. In this way, each general is a passer of information and receives ten messages (attack or retreat). Even if there are traitors, as long as more than half of the people are supporting attack, the operation can be successful. However, in this case, each general does not tell who is the source of the information; it cannot be traced back to the source, and it is difficult to find out who is the traitor in case of inconsistency.

2. Written agreement

Every general among these ten generals writes a letter to another nine generals. Let's suppose that General No. 1 writes "attack" and signs the letter. The other generals who received the letter can verify that this is indeed the signature of General No. 1. General No. 2 also decided to attack and attached his own vote to the letter of General No. 1, and wrote "attack" and signed his own name. If General No. 3 also agrees to attack, he will also attach an "attack" vote to the original letter and sign it.

When the letter is signed by six generals, an agreement to "attack" is reached. In comparison with the verbal agreement, the written one can help you to find the source of information and to reveal the generals who have agreed to attack. If they attack together, and those who have signed to attack will retreat during the attack, then the general is a traitor and he will be put to death during his retreat.

But here is also a problem with this written agreement: how to ensure that only one general at an exact time attaches his own content after the letter. In other words, after the letter of General No. 1 is sent out, only one general among General Nos. 2 to 10 can attach his signature and pass it on to another general.

In real life, there can be more than ten nodes in a distributed network. So how is a consensus mechanism designed in order to have a large number of nodes "sign" the order?

To design such a consensus mechanism, we must follow the basic design principle of distributed networks. This principle is called CAP (Consistency, Availability, and Partition Tolerance) theory.

2.2 CAP Theory

I like fish, and I also like bear's paws. If I cannot have the two together, I will let the fish go, and take the bear's paws.

These are famous words by Chinese Philosopher Mencius that tells us there are hard choices to make in our lives. In distributed systems, CAP theory is the "fish and bear's paw" problem that system designers can't escape.

CAP theory was proposed by the famous computer scientist Eric Allen Brewer in the late 1990s. Specifically, it says that Consistency, Availability, and Partition Tolerance cannot exist together in a distributed system. CAP theory advocates that any data sharing system in the network can only have maximum two of the following three conditions:

Consistency (C): all nodes access the same copy of the latest data, and all applications can access the same data at any time.

Availability (A): healthy nodes respond to the client's requests within a limited time, and there is no need to wait all the time.

Partition Tolerance (P): so-called partition means that the system cannot achieve data consistency within the time limit. Once this happens, a choice between C and A for the current operation must be made. You have to ensure that the cluster can continue to serve if some nodes in the cluster are disconnected.

Figure 2.1 represents the relationship between these three elements.

As shown in the figure, to satisfy CP, in the case of network partitioning, in order to achieve C, the request can only wait for a while, and as the result won't achieve A; if CA is to be achieved, the node status must be consistent within the time limit, and the network partition must not emerge, so it cannot satisfy AP. To satisfy AP, the separated nodes are serving simultaneously but cannot communicate with each other, which will result in inconsistent states and won't satisfy C.

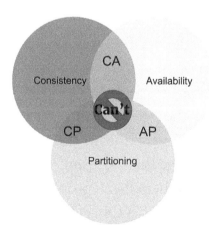

Figure 2.1   CAP Theory.

But in fact, there is no distributed system that can avoid network failure (P). Therefore, system architects often have to choose between satisfying CP and AP.

Limited by this theory, in 2008, Nakamoto discovered the Bitcoin and proposed the Proof-of-Work (PoW) workload proof mechanism, which became an ultimate solution to the Byzantine Generals problem.

2.3 PoW (Proof-of-Work) Mechanism

Bitcoin or bottom-layer blockchain technology, in fact is a public ledger that records real-time transactions in the Bitcoin network. This ledger needs constant data updates, so how to ensure the data accuracy on this ledger, and how to ensure that the entire network recognizes only this one ledger?

If we assume that there are 10 computers on the whole network, and the ledger should be updated every 10 minutes, then who's ledger will be considered as an accurate? The answer given by Nakamoto is that every update should be made only according to one computer. Which one? We do it according to the one who has completed the workload. This is the PoW mechanism. The workload here refers specifically to mining, that is, using computing power to solve a complex mathematical problem. The miner who solves it first and completes the "workload" can update the public ledger. After the miner updated the ledger, other people on the network would update it simultaneously.

(Note: If there are two miners who have completed the workload at the same time, then the network speed decides who will be the first: the one who will broadcast the first will get the right to record.)

So why are some people willing to complete the workload and maintain the consistency of the Bitcoin ledger?

The answer can be found in Nakamoto's whitepaper that miners who are involved in mining can get Bitcoin rewards. Each ledger update represents a reward of 50 bitcoins, which is halved every 4 years. There were 50 in 2009–2012, 25 in 2013–2016, and 12.5 will be in 2017–2020. This set of economic incentives allows more miners to participate, constantly update the ledger, and jointly maintain the stability of the Bitcoin network.

The core idea of Satoshi Nakamoto's PoW design is that you can be a traitor, you can do evil, you can make false accounts to destroy the stability of the entire network, but you must bear the relevant cost. Under the PoW mechanism, a person must complete more than 50% of the workload in the entire network in order to start an attack on it. This cost is enormous. It's better to follow the rules honestly and earn some bitcoin.

In the past decade since the birth of Bitcoin, as the number of network nodes has increased, the cost of launching attacks has become more and more expensive, and the PoW mechanism has been proven to be safe and reliable. However, in order to maintain the consistency of the ledger (C in CAP theory) and the system operation stability in case of such problems as a node drop in network partition (P), bitcoin network sacrifices availability (A) to some extent. Some people also call this problem "latency", the delay problem. The network needs 10 minutes to wait, and there should be enough transactions to be confirmed before the account can be updated. If Bitcoin is going to get the AP, the client should accept the transaction as soon as it is added to the blockchain, so that it does not need to depend on other nodes, and so that is very useful. But there is a risk that the remaining nodes may reject the transaction and thereby sacrifice the consistency.

In addition, many people think that the most important thing about money is safety. They believe that giving a lot of works to solve mathematical problems in order to ensure the safety of Bitcoin in the PoW mechanism is a wasteful behavior. Here, we will talk about three major issues of the PoW mechanism, which are often discussed by the community.

2.3.1 Problem of PoW 1: Waste of Resources

Iceland is known as a "miner's paradise". The temperature there is cold, a computer server can be naturally cooled, and the renewable energy of geothermal and hydroelectric power plants makes the electricity price lower; in that way it attracts bitcoin mining companies from all over the world.

In mid-February 2018, a number of overseas media reported that the electricity used for mining in Iceland in 2018 would exceed the total household electricity consumption of the country's 340,000 population. A week later, the Elite Fixtures website published an updated bitcoin mining cost survey of that week. The results showed that to mine one bitcoin, the average electricity consumption of Antminer S9 mine was 17,773 kW, the electricity consumption of S7 was 45,889 kW, and the electricity consumption of Avalon 6 was 55,294 kW. A lot of media don't understand what is Bitcoin mining; they just track the hot spots, as was with the "electricity consumption". They used the words "shock!" and "terrible!" to emphasize that the consumption of energy for mining was huge.

Bitmain, the leader of the Bitcoin mining manufacturers, has never publicly stated its position on energy consumption. In 2018, I talked to a famous Chinese economist Buer Feimo about mining problems; Mr. Bu's answer about whether mining power consumption can be defined as wasteful behavior was very simple and sharp: "I spend my own money on the electricity which I want to consume by myself. This is simple consumer behavior. How can it be wasteful?"

The PoW mechanism is also applied by Ethereum, the second-largest cryptocurrency in terms of market capitalization. But the founder of Ethereum, Vitalik Buterin, also hopes to modify the consensus mechanism. When I asked him why, he replied: "I personally feel that PoW wastes energy and has bad influence on the environment. Now the electricity consumption for mining Bitcoin is equivalent to the electricity consumption of the whole Singapore.

And Ethereum electricity consumption currently reaches 30% of Singapore's total electricity consumption".

I have forwarded the opinion of the economist about wasting resources to Vitalik Buterin. He refuted in this way: "From social point of view, it is indeed a wasteful behavior. But from the standpoint of miners it is not wasting of resources".

In fact, if any consumer behavior is raised to the level of the society, the problem will be more complicated.

2.3.2 Problem of PoW 2: Environmental Problem

Last December, CNNMoney reported that some experts said that Bitcoin mining consumes a lot of energy and may be harmful to the environment. For example, meteorologist Eric Holthaus believes that Bitcoin mining is slowing the transition of fossil fuels to renewable energy and eventually consumes more electricity than is available. Environmentalists are not outdone as well, and they are afraid that bitcoin mining will seriously harm global efforts to combat climate change.

In January, Credit Suisse in its latest report mentioned that bitcoin mining is unlikely to cause an "environmental Armageddon". That report said, "it is a mistake to project miners' power consumption lineally, as the industry will likely develop hardware and practices that are more energy-efficient in a bid to gain a competitive advantage. The report noted that this phenomenon occurred among both marijuana growers and data center operators during high-growth periods for these industries".[1]

Of course, the argument of polluting the environment can provide new business opportunities for the industry. Now companies have begun to research green mining.

Last December, I received an email from the United States. A traditional company said they were researching green mining and asked me to give them contact of Chinese mining machine manufacturers for potential business cooperation. I checked it out at their official website, but I did not find out that they are related to mining business, so I refused their request. In February 2018, I saw a website reporting that a Bitcoin ATM producer is also entering the green mining industry. According to the company, "it is possible to run these machines solely on renewable energy without losing performance".[2] If you search for "green bitcoin mining" on Google, you can find that many companies have expressed that they can provide green mining solutions, and there is a company who has developed a solar-powered mining machine.

The cost of these green mining solutions is higher than the cost of traditional hydropower or thermal power. Therefore, even if there is a possibility of green mining, the miners will still leave the things as they are.

---

[1] https://www.ccn.com/bitcoin-mining-isnt-environmental-armageddon-credit-suisse-report.
[2] https://cointelegraph.com/news/green-mining-company-to-reduce-coin-generating-energy-costs-by-harnessing-renewable-power.

2.3.3 Problem of PoW 3: Centralization of Computing Power

Bitcoin has experienced hundreds of "deaths" during last 10 years since its birth. Besides from external factors, there can be only an internal cause for the real death of Bitcoin. There is a sword of Damocles hanging over the "head" of Bitcoin and that is "51% power attack". Here, we can understand the power as a workload. In other words, whoever completes the workload of more than 50% of the entire network, whoever has the whole, decides the flow of bitcoin transactions, establishes new rules, and reaches a new consensus. As it is shown in Figure 2.2, now, only mainland China is a computing power of more than 40% of the entire network.

I have privately teased my friends that the Bitmain is a "mysterious force from the East" which the Western world is not able to understand. How has this mysterious force risen?

In August 2012, Jiang Xinyu (Internet nickname is "fried-cat") from Chinese Science and Technology University set up a company in Shenzhen. He announced to manufacture Application Specific Integrated Circuit (ASIC) mining machines, and fundraised online through a "virtual IPO" project, which was issued with a price of 0.1 bitcoin. He issued 160,000 shares and promised that those who bought the stocks could be paid with dividends. Wu Jihan, CEO of Bitmain, bought 15,000 virtual stocks. After that, two things happened that made Wu Jihan realize the importance of obtaining bitcoin mining technology.

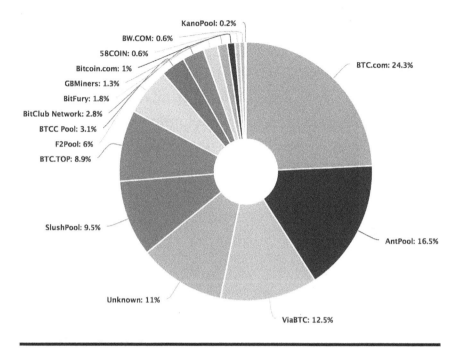

Figure 2.2 Bitcoin Hashrate Distribution. (Note: both Antpool and BTC.com belong to Bitmain.) https://www.mangoresearch. co/understanding-blockchain-tech-cap-theorem/.

In December 2012, "friedcat" called Wu Jihan and told him that something went wrong with the ASIC chip. The problem was solved later, which was a huge relief to Jihan.

In April 2013, Wu Jihan spent several millions for the Avalon mining machine pre-order. But the delivery was not on time to the delivery date. We must realize that miners would suffer great if their mining machines were delayed in shipping while hashrate increases in the network. The result would be disastrous.

After these two experiences, Wu Jihan created Bitmain in May 2013. In the late May of the same year, CCTV's "Half-hour Economy" reported bitcoin news for the first time and attracted a large number of investors to enter the market, which gave birth to a huge mining machine market. Two months later, there emerged a multiple bitcoin miners: Pigeon, TMR, Biter, Landchip, Bee, Garden, Smart, etc.

In the fierce competition, Wu Jihan's technical partner Micree Zhan independently developed the first generation of Bitmain Antminer machines S1 in less than 6 months after their company had been established. The energy consumption of the same computing power was half less in comparison with the previous mining machine. At the beginning of 2015, Zhan Ketuan developed and launched the fifth-generation Bitmain Antminer S5, which established the leading position of Bitmain in the mining market. Bitmain Antminer machines evolved fast and became a new game changer.

In fact, a close review of the history of the development of Chinese mining machine manufacturers in the early years can show that there is a great similarity with the current ICO boom. There also have been various kinds of chaos such as postponed deliveries, scams, and illegal fundraising, which were checking the credibility of people in the industry. Yang Haipo, the founder of Viabtc, once sighed: "There are a lot of mining machines manufacturers which existed at the same time with Bitmain, but later on they all got into bankruptcy. Mining machine manufacturing requires coordination of procurement, supply chain, logistics and other aspects. The success of Bitmain shows that Wu Jihan is an excellent 'steersman' of the company".

On February 24, 2018, CNBC quoted analytics company Bernstein that Bitmain's revenue in 2017 was as high as $3 billion to $4 billion, equivalent to Nvidia's last year's profit. The Bernstein's analysts mentioned in their report: "But Bitmain achieved this in merely 4 years, while it took Nvidia 24 years to get here".[3]

The report "Bitmain madly earned $3 billion, and it rivals Nvidia" has occupied the headlines of various traditional media and blockchain media in China and abroad for a while. This article sparked a discussion about whether the mining industry had a huge profit problem and divided it into two groups with clear positions. One group insisted that Bitmain is monopolizing the mining machine market and is trying to control bitcoin; the other group embraced Bitcoin, emphasizing that this is the result of market competition.

Huang Shiliang (official WeChat account is Lightning HSL), a well-known blockchain educator in China, believes that "the more expensive the mining machine, the better it is. The more expensive is the price, the more it indicates the contribution of Wu Jihan to this industry". But he also admitted that Bitmain is now a "unicorn" in the mining industry. Analyst Berstein estimates that Bitmain occupies a 70%–80% share of the Bitcoin mining machines and ASICS chip market.

---

[3] https://www.cnbc.com/2018/02/23/secretive-chinese-bitcoin-mining-company-may-have-made-as-much-money-as-nvidia-last-year.html.

For this reason, the community called for the changes in the consensus algorithm, hoping that more miners will participate and break the monopoly of Bitmain.

Can you defeat this unicorn only by modifying the consensus algorithm?

Zhu Fa, co-founder of Poolin, believes that the changes in bitcoin algorithm are a pit: "First of all, if the BTC does not use SHA256 (hash algorithm), then the SHA256 computing power will immediately switch to other currencies with the same algorithm, such as BCH, SBTC. As a result, the BTC holder would be 'trapped'. Secondly, after the algorithm is changed, basically the first thing is to make a new algorithm for the mining machine. So BTC miner has to re-purchase the mining machine. Miners will suffer losses. Thirdly, if ASIC-unfriendly algorithms are used as Monero and Ethereum do, it will make community resources and value flow towards other currencies, such as Monero and Ethereum. As a result, BTC holders would suffer losses".

Vitalik Buterin, a founder of Ethereum, tweeted a hybrid PoW/PoS system.[4]

Vitalik wasn't the first to propose this hybrid consensus mechanism of PoW+PoS. As early as in 2012, a geek with pseudonym Sunny King invented Peercoin and first adopted the Proof-of-Stake (PoS) mechanism to maintain network security.

---

[4] https://www.computerworld.com/article/3299697/what-vitalik-buterin-tweet-storm-means-for-future-ethereum-blockchain.html

2.4 PoS (Proof-of-Stake) Mechanism

PoS is Proof-of-Stake. Stake means rights and interests, and as to the interests, each holder is a stakeholder. With the PoW mechanism, consensus is reached when someone has completed the workload and update the ledger. With the PoS mechanism, token holders with the largest tokens have more voices in the system. The latter is obviously more efficient than the former and can save a lot of power.

Therefore, Ethereum also planned to switch from PoW mechanism to PoW+PoS.

At this level, whales have more sayings in the PoS mechanisms than simple users. It seems rather unfair. This is like when a company makes a decision, the final decision is up to shareholders who has more equities. If so, how do you attract more new people to participate?

Vitalik said that PoW has the same problem of insufficient attraction for new users. He suggested new users start with Dapps like CryptoKitties to participate in the system.

This answer does not seem to be convincing. Dapps like CryptoKitties can be developed in Ethereum, and they could also be developed and applied in Bitcoin. So, which one is more attractive to new users?

As we mentioned above, Bitmain made $3 billion–$4 billion in 2017, and it was achieved in 4 years, while it took Nvidia 24 years. I believe that many people would be attracted by the lure of huge wealth and are eager to tap into this industry. Japanese Internet giant GMO is working on a 7 nm mining chip; Samsung, a leading electronics company in South Korea, is also producing ASIC chips and supplies products to the Chinese mining companies.

Therefore, when we discuss the monopoly of Bitmain, we must not ignore the fact that the market is constantly evolving, and there always will be new companies to compete with Bitmain. But can PoS mechanism evolve in this way?

There is "resource curse" theory in the economics. It means that rich natural resources may rather be a "curse" of economic development than a "blessing". Under the PoS mechanism, no matter how the market evolves, big whales can always get more rewards if they can find the way to remain an upper hand. It's a dead end that the rich get richer and the poor get poorer. This kind of consensus approach can lead to strong centralization, which seems to be contrary to the decentralized spirit of the blockchain.

2.5 LPoS (Leased Proof-of-Stake) Mechanism

It's the same situation as with PoW mechanism; miners with less computing power can't compete with miners own huge hashrate. With PoS mechanism, users with less tokens can't compete with the big token holders for the right to record on the ledger, so they lack motivation to operate on the network nodes.

This means that the entire network is only maintained by a few big whales. Only if there are more network nodes, more people participate, and the network can be more secure, so it is necessary to encourage small players to participate. Leased Proof-of-Stake (LPoS) allows simple users to lend their own coins to other nodes, increasing the weight of this node in the network. If the node can add the transaction to the public ledger, the proceeds will be shared to the original holder in an exact proportion.

2.6 DPoS (Delegated Proof-of-Stake) Mechanism

DPoS is a delegated Proof-of-Stake mechanism. DPoS is based on the PoS, and there is one more option added – being "delegated". Those who can get the right to (record on the ledger) are elected by the community and are rotated. This is similar to the National People's Congress (NPC) system. We vote to select those who can represent the interests of the community as a whole, and if the representative does not perform well (e.g., do not record on time), we can also replace him. DPoS mechanism is relatively more decentralized compared with PoS mechanism.

In fact, all mathematical programs are the simulations of the real world, and this mechanism of representative elections is the best mechanism that is proved to be the best in work. We can regard the elected representatives as "elites", and this mechanism can be regarded as an elite agent system.

It doesn't matter whether it is PoW, PoS, LPoS, or DPoS, they follow the same rule: the one who does more work gets more coins. If one can be elected as representative, doesn't that mean he is better than others in some ways? Is it that he must have completed a specific "workload" in the past, so he has got today's achievements? Can we simply regard various consensus mechanisms as a product at the market? Existence is justified, and when it is adopted, there is a market. The most important thing is to develop your own products, not to "hurt" others maliciously.

In the past few years, there has been developing many consensus mechanisms in the community, especially, the creative consensus inventions of various ICO projects. No matter which consensus mechanism it is, as long as it can generate demand and get more people involved, it is a valuable mechanism. We welcome the various consensus mechanisms to compete with each other and let the market decide the winners.

Readers can also use their imagination to design new consensus mechanisms, such as proof-of-reputation; everything is up to the one who has a good reputation; proof-of-credits, everything is up to one who has the highest credit limit.

Chapter 3

Optimized Consensus Mechanism

3.1 Optimized Versions of PoW Mechanism

We all know that Bitcoin's PoW uses SHA256 algorithm. Initially, individuals can participate in mining through CPU. However, when chip manufacturers such as Bitmain and Avalon developed ASIC, mining is not something that individuals can do easily. Later, with the emergence of graphic card mining and mining pools, the Bitcoin community began to worry that the mining pool would result in concentration of computing power, contrary to the original design concept of "one CPU, one ticket". During that time, the anxiety of centralization was very serious. The discussion in the Bitcoin community was very intense. Bitcoin was "dead" again and again in the forum. Until now, the debates over whether the mining pool violates the principle of decentralization are continuing.

3.1.1 Litecoin's SCRYPT Algorithm

SHA256 algorithm was one of the reasons people thought that led to professional mining machines and mining pools, since this algorithm could be easily computed. Therefore, people started to look for better algorithms.

At that time, Litecoin emerged, and it was based on the SCRYPT algorithm. It is said that SCRYPT was developed by a well-known hacker and has not been widely used because it has not received strict security review and comprehensive arguments such as the SHA series. Compared with the SHA256 algorithm, SCRYPT has higher hardware requirements, occupies more memory, and consumes more computing time. Parallel computing is extremely difficult. Obviously, the SCRYPT algorithm is more resistant to mining. In addition, Litecoin changed the block time to 2.5 minutes. In the era when the altcoin was still rare, the Litecoin relied on these two innovations to achieve great success and took the first position from the altcoin for a long time.

Later, SCRYPT algorithm was modified into SCRYPT-N algorithm, which improved the general idea. They all pursued greater memory consumption and calculation time to hold back ASIC mining machine.

Soon, the success of Litecoin induced a variety of algorithmic innovations. Between 2012 and 2014, algorithmic innovation has always been a hot topic in community discussions, and every currency that uses innovative algorithms can make a new wave.

3.1.2 *Tandem and Dash*

Rearranging combinations is the most common method among the innovative methods that are commonly used by humans. In addition to the idea of increasing memory consumption and increasing of the computation time, some people began to think: "Can you use multiple hash algorithms instead of just a single algorithm"?

So, in July 2013, Quark was released, and it was the first use of multiple rounds of hash algorithm. It sounded like a very high-level thing, but in fact it was very simple and was to do nine rounds of hash operation on the input data, and the previous round of results was used as the input of the next round of operations. These six encryption algorithms used in these nine rounds of hashing were BLAKE, BMW, GROESTL, JH, KECCAK, and SKEIN, all of which were well-recognized secure hash algorithms, and implementation code had already existed.

When this multi-round hashing method has appeared, it gave people a visually safe and powerful feeling, and there were countless fans.

Dash (DASH, formerly Darkcoin) is based on this micro-innovation, it uses 11 algorithms: BLAKE, BMW, GROESTL, JH, KECCAK, SKEIN, LUFFA, CUBEHASH, SHAVITE, SIMD, ECHO, and it is called X11. Then, later emerged X13, X15 series.

This kind of algorithm is actually a serial idea. The drawback is that as long as one of the algorithms is cracked, the whole algorithm is cracked. It is like an interlocking chain: as long as one of the rings is broken, the whole chain is divided into two.

3.1.3 Parallel Algorithm and Heavycoin

In case of tandem, it is natural to think of parallelism, and Heavycoin (HVC) was the first to try. Although it is now unknown in the country, it was the first time when the game was implemented on chain and it can be described as famous.

Details of HVC algorithm:

1. Input data, perform a HEFTY1 hash operation, and get the result d1.
2. Take d1 as input, then perform SHA256, KECCAK512, GROESTL512, and BLAKE512 operations in turn, and obtain outputs d2, d3, d4, and d5 separately.
3. Finally, the first 64 bits of d2–d5 are extracted separately, and the final 256-bit hash result is formed as the block ID.

Why should we first perform a round of HEFTY1 hashing? The reason is that HEFTY1 is extremely difficult to calculate and its resistance against mining machines exceeds SCRYPT. But like SCRYPT, security has not been justified by an official agency, so the latter four security-recognized algorithms have been added to enhance security.

Let's compare the methods of series connection and parallel connection of algorithms. Series connection methods such as Quark, X11, X13, etc., use a variety of hash functions in a series connection, but do not improve the overall collision resistance, because their securities are determined by the weakest algorithm. As soon as any weak hash function encounters a collision attack, it endangers the security of the whole system (Figure 3.1).

Let's take a look at the parallel connection algorithm HVC; it extracts 64 bits from SHA256, KECCAK512, GROESTL512, and BLAKE512 algorithms separately and get the final result after fusion and confusion. If one of the

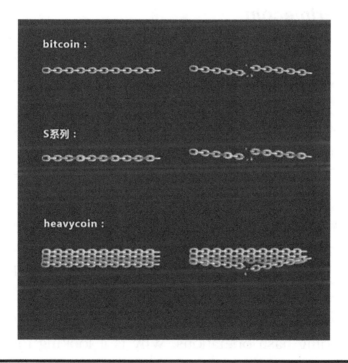

Figure 3.1 Different Algorithm Structure. (*Source*: The original figure is taken from the evolution of blockchain core technology of CSDN – algorithm evolution), https://www.beekuaibao.com/article/606092600472616960

algorithms was cracked, it can only endanger one of 64 bits, and only if the four algorithms are cracked at the same time, it will endanger the whole system.

Bitcoin uses only one type of hash algorithm. Imagine that when SHA256 proves to be no longer secure on a certain day, although the algorithm can be changed, it will inevitably lead to unstableness of the system. If you use the parallel algorithm, you can gain a relative stable period for hard fork transition.

3.1.4 Primecoin

While some people are constantly exploring algorithms, others are accusing PoW of wasting energy, PoS mechanism has already been implemented. Although people who support PoW are trying to maintain it, but they have to admit the fact that PoW consumes energy. This accusation opens up another path of exploration, which is perfect if you can find an algorithm that can maintain blockchain security and generate value in other ways.

The most inspiring result on this way of exploration is Primecoin. It was invented by Sunny King (pseudonym), who also developed Peercoin. The core idea of the prime currency algorithm is to look for large prime numbers while doing hash operations. Why is it looking for prime numbers? Because the prime numbers are rare on the number axis and the distribution is irregular, finding the prime numbers on the number axis can be only blindly searched and explored, which is the characteristic of the PoW.

Another requirement of PoW is to be verified easily. In this case, people have achieved some results after hundreds of years of exploration. The Primecoin is tested in two ways: first by the Fermat test and then by the Euler–Lagrange–Lipschitz test; if both tests pass, it can be considered as a prime number. It should be pointed out that this method does not guarantee that hundreds of passes through the test are all prime numbers, but which does not affect the system operation. Even if the test results are wrong, as long as every node considers it as a prime number, the system will work.

Primecoin is actually looking for Cunningham chains.

There are three specific types of Cunningham chains: type one Cunningham chain, type two Cunningham chain, and bi-twin chain.

What is Cunningham chain? Let's use the example of the first type of Cunningham chain to explain.

Each number in the Cunningham chain is twice the previous number minus one, such as

1531, 3061, 6121, 12241, 24481

The next number of numbers in the series 48961 (24481 * 2 − 1) is not a prime number, so the length of this Cunningham chain is 5, and the goal of Primecoin is to explore a longer Cunningham chain (all three categories are OK).

So here is the most important question. How can I use the Cunningham chain to verify that a block is legit?

Let's take a look at the implementation details of Primecoins.

1. Hashing Satoshi Nakamoto's block head: hashBlockHeader = SHA256(BlockHeader)
2. Get the first number of the Cunningham chain by transformation: originNum = hashBlockHeader * Multiplier

After obtaining the first number of the originNum of the Cunningham's chain, the integer part of the length of the prime chain can be tested and calculated, and the calculation of the fractional part is related to the span of the last non-prime of the Cunningham's chain.

Multiplexing of each block is different, and the calculation process is related to the hashBlockHeader. For this purpose, the Primecoin has been modified specifically for the block header, and field bnPrimeChainMultiplier has been added to store the product factor. However, when the hashBlockHeader is calculated in the first step above, the input data does not contain this product factor, and that is why the Satoshi Nakamoto's block is specifically pointed out.

Primecoin is the first cryptocurrency on the market that does not use the Hash workload proof mechanism. The mining process itself has a certain scientific value. But why are you not getting a big promotion?

According to the knowledge we have, the prime numbers are unevenly distributed on the numerical axis, and the larger the number, the rarer the prime numbers. The difficulty of finding is not linearly increasing, so the time consumption is unpredictable. However, the blockchain requires block stability, and the prime number algorithm is not popular. But this kind of exploration is not meaningless, and the exploration of using the workload of PoW is still going on.

3.1.5 Ethash and Ethereum

Ethereum originally intended to use PoS, but due to some problems with PoS design, the development team decided to use the PoW method in the Ethereum 1.0 phase. Then in the Serenity phase, Ethereum will be converted from PoW to PoS. Proof-of-work (PoW) means converting electricity to heat, Ethash and network stability.

Ethereum's PoW algorithm is called Ethash (a modified version of the Dagger-Hashimoto algorithm), which is slightly different from Bitcoin's PoW algorithm, which makes it possible to mine with ordinary hardware.

The latest version of Ethash is designed to meet the following goals:

1. IO saturation: the algorithm should consume almost the entire available memory access bandwidth, which is a strategy to achieve ASIC resistance, which is aimed at available RAM, especially in GPUs VRAM, and comparing to computers' memory, it is closer to the theoretically optimal value)
2. "GPU-friendly": make GPU mining as simple as possible. It is almost impossible for the CPU mining

because the potential specialization impacts are too huge, and the CPU-friendly algorithms do have the disadvantage of being vulnerable to botnet attacks. So after comprehensive consideration, it was chosen to be "GPU - Graphics Processing Unit friendly".

3. Light client verifiability: light clients should be able to verify a round of mining in 0.01 second units on a C language desktop, and verify a round of mining in Python or JavaScript; verification of one round of mining in 0.1 second units will require 1 MB of memory (but exponentially).

4. Light client slowdown: the process of running algorithms with a light client should be much slower than using a full client, so running algorithms on light clients (including through dedicated hardware) is not an economically viable way to mine.

5. Light client quick start: light client should be able to operate completely and be able to verify blocks in JavaScript in 40 seconds

By these considerations, the Ethash mining that was finally released by the development team was basically independent of CPU performance, but was positively related to memory size and memory bandwidth. This workload proof algorithm from Ethereum reduces the efficiency of specific hardware ASICs that is commonly used for Bitcoin mining.

The basic process of the Ethash algorithm is given as follows:

For each block, first calculate a seed by scanning the block header: the seed is only related to the information of the current block; use the seed to generate a 16 MB pseudo-random data set (cache); and then, generate a 1 GB data set – the DAG based on the cache. Each element in this data set depends only on a few elements in the cache. In other words, as long as there is a cache, you can quickly calculate the elements in the specified position in the DAG. DAG can be understood as a complete search space. The mining process is to select elements from the DAG randomly (similar to finding the appropriate Nonce in Bitcoin mining) and then perform the hash operation.

The verification process is similar. It gets the specified position of the element, based on the cache to get, and then, it verifies that the hash result of this set of elements is less than a certain value. The verification process only needs to be done with normal CPU and normal memory. This is because the cache is small, and the DAG elements at the specified location are easy to compute. Cache and DAG are updated every 30,000 blocks.

3.1.6 Equihash and Zcash

In October 2016, Zcash went online. The biggest feature of that currency was the usage of a zero-knowledge proof to achieve private transactions. The zero-knowledge proof gives the proof without leaking the information, and the verifier confirms whether it is correct by verifying it. Zcash hides all the information of the trader in the blockchain record, including the address of the two parties and the amount of the transaction, thus achieving anonymity. Zcash was very cautious about the choice of algorithm. After considering the algorithms such as SHA256D, SCRYPT, CUCKOO HASH, and LYRA2, Zcash team has chosen Equihash.

Equihash is a PoW algorithm designed by Alex Biryukov and Dmitry Khovratovich. The theoretical basis is computer science and an issue in cryptography – a generalized birthday paradox. Equihash is a memory-dependent algorithm. The size of the computing power depends mainly on how much memory it has. It is more suitable for general-purpose computers with a large amount of memory, rather than special hardware chips. According to the papers of two inventors, the algorithm requires at least 700M of memory and a 1.8 GHz CPU for 30 seconds. After optimization by the Zcash project, each mining thread currently needs 1G memory, so Zcash officially believes that the algorithm is difficult to appear in the short-term mining machine (ASIC) and thus achieves the ASIC resistance against the performance of the mining machine. Because the generalized birthday paradox has been extensively studied, Zcash officially believes that the algorithm is fair, and they think it is difficult for someone or an organization to optimize the algorithm secretly. The Equihash algorithm is very easy to verify, which is very important for implementing Zcash light clients on restricted devices in the future. The general process of Zcash mining is: first construct the input conditions (block head and various parameters), then transform the input conditions into "general form of generalized birthday problem" through a specific function, then use the optimization algorithm to solve the problem, and obtain the solution. And then, estimate the difficulty of the received solution. If the algorithm condition and the difficulty condition are fulfilled at the same time, it is determined that the "mining" is successful; otherwise, the random number is to be recomputed.

Chinese bitcoingold (BTG) is also using the Equihash algorithm. BTG is also a branch of the Bitcoin blockchain. BTG miners created blocks in Bitcoin block 491407 with a new work-proving algorithm and forked it successfully, in the area before Bitcoin block 491407 the blockchain remained unchanged. The original token allocation method for BTG is almost identical to the one used for Bitcoin cash forks on August 1. When the block 491406 is forked, the owner holding the Bitcoin automatically receives the BTG at a rate of 1 BTC = 1 BTG.

3.2 Optimized PoS

3.2.1 Byzantine General and Byzantine Fault-Tolerance Algorithm

In 1982, Lamport, Shostak, and Pease first raised the issue of General Byzantine. Ethan Buchman from Cosmos describes: "This is a problem with implementing a distributed protocol in a compromised communication network, that is, the problem of building a reliable system in an unreliable environment". Since then, no one has been able to create a system that can solve the problem of Byzantine Generals from 1982 to 1999. Because at that time, the Internet just evolved from cloud-based central computing, all that needed to be solved was fault tolerance. Therefore, in the people's consciousness, the Byzantine General problem is irrelevant to the calculation, and more is the popularity of fault-tolerant algorithms. For example, the Paxos algorithm invented in 1998 and the Raft algorithm invented in 2013 are widely used. The Practical Byzantine Fault Tolerance (PBFT) was invented in 1999, in addition to the academic world, and has not been widely used in real life.

Until 2008, when Satoshi Nakamoto designed the distributed Byzantine Fault Tolerance (BFT) algorithm at the network scale level into the blockchain solution, which popularized BFT. Since then, people in the computing systems research community have begun to conceive how to apply BFT to the real world.

In 2011, the BitcoinTalk Forum organized a discussion on the concept of proof-of-stake (PoS). The original PoS study assumes that a series of peer nodes in the system are static and stable for a long time. But this assumption in the blockchain environment is completely unrealistic. Therefore, the initial PoS protocol implementation results are not ideal. Until the creation of Tendermint by Jae Kwon in 2014, when it was the first truly applied distributed BFT study to the PoS public blockchain environment. A major breakthrough for Jae Kwon is to enable Tendermint to apply BFT research to the field of replication state machines (blockchains) using block, hash links, dynamic validator sets, and loop leader elections. In the Tendermint environment, a large number of consensus algorithms (Honeybadger, Ouroboros, Tezos, Casper) are applied, all of which contain elements of BTF research and elements observed by other modules in the blockchain.

In fact, all the research done for proof-of-entitlement (PoS) points to an important question: Can we achieve the level of security for the PoW without running out of scarce material resources? This problem can be translated into: PoS voting rights are not calculated by calculation but are denominated in the currency of the chain.

In comparison with the scalability of the blockchain, the discussion of the PoS consensus issue of blockchain is more extensive and enthusiastic. Due to the high cost of running PoW mining and various external environmental issues, a large amount of resources is pouring into PoS security research.

3.2.2 Algorithm for Realizing Proof-of-Stake

Next, we will discuss the three main PoS protocols that use PoS in cryptocurrencies:

- CTFG (Casper the Friendly Ghost) – research led by Vlad Zamfir

■ CFFG (Casper the Friendly Finality Gadget) – research led by Vitalik Buterin

■ Tendermint – research led by Jae Kwon.

There are many different ways to implement PoS algorithms, but the two main principles of PoS design are chain-based PoS and BFT based on PoS. Tendermint is based on the Byzantine fault-tolerant PoS design, CTFG is a chain-based PoS design, and CFFG is a mixture of both.

The CAP theory in computer science returns the impossibility of providing more than two-thirds of guarantees in distributed data systems: Availability, Consistency, and Partition Tolerance. Chain-based PoS algorithms tend to choose high availability without high consistency, because high availability means that all transactions can be processed, but at the expense of consistent state replication across the network. BFT-based, on the other hand, tends to choose high consistency.

(1) Tendermint and PoS Based on BTF

In PFT-based PoS protocol pseudo-random arrangements, a verifier proposes a block during multiple rounds of voting. However, committing and finalizing blocks depends on the majority $-2/3$ of all verifiers sign on the submitted block. It may take several rounds before the block is finalized. The BFT system can only fail $1/3$ of the failures, including failures or malicious attacks.

Tendermint consists of two main technologies: the blockchain consensus engine and a common application interface. The consensus engine is called the Tendermint core module, ensuring that the same transactions are recorded in the same order in each machine. The application interface is called the Application Blockchain Interface (ABCI), allowing transactions to be processed by programs written in any programming language.

In the core module, Tendermint works based on a circular voting mechanism, which is also the principle of a consensus protocol. A round is divided into three processing steps: the verifier proposes a block, sends the submission intent, and submits a new block after signing. This mechanism provides a secure state replicator for atomic broadcasts, adding a layer of responsibility – a security failure can be completely attributed to Tendermint.

The Tendermint consensus algorithm starts with a set of verifiers. The verifier maintains a full copy of the blockchain and can use the public key to identify the certifier's identity. They took turns to propose a block.

Only one verifier can propose a block for each round of voting, and this should be signed with the verifier's corresponding private key, so if there is an error, the verifier responsible for this can be found. Then, the remaining certifiers need to vote for each proposal, and the votes need to be signed with their own private key. These make up a round. However, it may take several rounds to submit a new block because of the asynchronous network, which is shown in Figure 3.2.

The certifier may fail while submitting block: current proposal may be offline, or network may experience

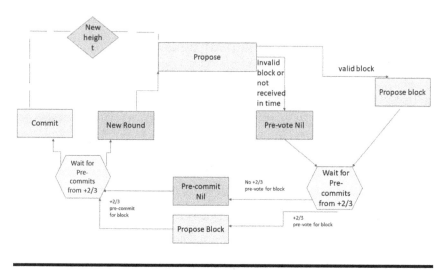

Figure 3.2 Casper vs. Tendermint. (*Source*: Medium "Consensus Compare: Casper vs. Tendermint".)

a delay. Tendermint allows the verifier to be escaped (when the turn comes to a verifier, the verifier is not creating a block). The verifier waits a short period of time to receive the entire block proposed by the proposer (the certifier of this round of the block) before moving to the next round of voting. This dependency on timeouts makes Tendermint a weak synchronization protocol rather than an asynchronous protocol. However, the multiplied protocol is asynchronous, and the verifier will only process if it receives more than two-thirds of the verifier set messages. Because of this, Tendermint requires most of the certifiers to function properly, and if one-third or more of the certifiers are offline or offline, the network will stop working.

Assuming less than one-third of the verifiers are Byzantium, Tendermint guarantees that security will never be compromised – it means that the verifier (more than 2/3) will never commit a conflicting block at the same height. Therefore, the blockchain based on Tendermint will never fork.

Nowadays, Tendermint's design decisions have placed security and immutability on the top of flexibility. There is a high probability in the real world that the system will really stop running and participants will need to restart the system after updating the software outside the protocol.

Only a few people in the digital cryptocurrency community understood Casper and why it was valuable, Tendermint laid the foundation for Casper research. The insight is that if a chain is itself highly fault-tolerant, then you can rely on the chain to make a good decision about who will make the block, but if the chain itself is unreliable, then you fall into the trap. The problem with chickens and eggs has gone, which used to be the catastrophe of all other consensus algorithms.

This design solution is considered to be inferior to available prior protocols such as Ethereum and Bitcoin. But we need to consider how to get back to the right chain in case if we have shifted to the unsafe chain.

Let's take a look at the trade-offs in Bitcoin: if its network is split, Bitcoin loses its security guarantee in the case of various attacks. This is actually an unmodifiable theory; that is, when your confidence interval is 100%, you are following a correct chain, and you will use this chain to choose who will produce the next block, but once you transfer from an insecure chain, there is no clear path to get you back to the right chain.

Clear features of Tendermint:

- Proven activity
- Security threshold: 1/3 of the verifier
- Public/private chain compatibility
- Instant final determinism: 1–3 seconds, depending on the number of certifiers
- Consistency first
- Consensus security on weakly synchronic networks.

(2) CFFG

The chain-based PoS imitates the workload proof consensus algorithm, in which the protocol allows the pseudo-randomly selected verifier to generate a new block, a hash join of the new block (including the hash value of the previous block) to the previous longest chain of the parent block. Chain-based PoS relies a lot on synchronous networks and usually prioritizes availability rather than consistency. Casper(s) is an adaptation of Tendermint's core ideas for environments that tend to be active rather than safe.

CTFG is a well-defined PoS construction, but CFFG is a PoS that covers the existing Ethereum PoW proposal mechanism, in fact combining both PoW and PoS.

Both Bitcoin and Ethereum's PoW Consensus Agreement will not make a "final" decision, and blocks may be potentially reorganized to some past block heights. When the block has no chance to be modified, it can be called "final determination".

Because the workload proof does not provide such a modification guarantee, it is considered to be unsafe. Conversely, when we continue to lengthen the chain, the final deterministic probability of the block is getting higher and higher. The logic implemented by CFFG can increase the desired final determination and 51% attack resistance for the Ethereum blockchain.

CFFG will be rolled out in multiple steps, and PoW security model is gradually transited to PoS security mode in a conservative manner. The first iteration of Casper will be to implement the hybrid PoW/PoS protocol discussed here. The last iteration of Casper is likely to draw on the lessons of CFFG and CTFG towards a complete PoS protocol.

CFFG is a hybrid between chain-based PoS and BFT-based PoS because it draws on both ideas. Its modular overlay design makes it easier to update the current PoW chain as it is a more conservative approach to upgrading the system to a completely different consensus model.

Casper's application logic exists inside smart contracts. To be a certifier in Casper, you must have Ethereum token (ETH) and store ETH in the Casper Smart Contract as a leveraged benefit. The mechanism proposed by the block in the first iteration of Casper will be preserved: it still uses the Nakamoto PoW consensus, and miners can create the blocks. However, in order to finalize the block, Casper's PoS coverage has control and has its own verifier to vote after the PoW miners.

One of the most important parts of Casper's PoS consensus is checkpoints. When Casper evaluates the final certainty in the 50-block increment, it is called a checkpoint, and every 50 block fragments is called an epoch. This process is triggered by the verifier who is sending a voting message at every cycle.

Just to sum up, the final determination of a block requires two conditions:

■ Most (more than 2/3) verifiers voted for block 1 during cycle 1 and therefore recognize block 1 as legit.
■ Most (more than 2/3) verifiers voted for block 2 during cycle 2, and block 2 is a sub-block of block 1, so block 1 was finalized during cycle 2

In the ideal implementation, the final determination of a block is carried out according to the following steps (check Figure 3.3):

2/3 vote for Block 1 → Judgment of Block 1 → 2/3 Voting Block for Block 2 → Final Determination for Block 1
Block 2 is a sub-block of block 1.

When a checkpoint is finalized, the verifier gets paid. However, if there are two finalized checkpoints that are split at the same height, then the security is broken, and at this time, the conditions for the reduction are reached, and at least 1/3 of the margin will be eliminated. When the

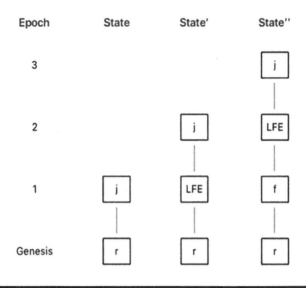

Figure 3.3   Final Block Determination Steps of Casper. (*Source*: Medium "Consensus Compare: Casper vs. Tendermint".)

security is compromised, evidence of the error attribution can be broadcasted as a transaction to the PoW miner. Then, PoW combines the evidence transaction into a block for mining, and the verifier who submitted the evidence will get the cost of the finder. When this happens, malicious verifiers signed in the conflict zone will be eliminated on both links, ensuring the legitimacy of the entire blockchain.

Now what happens if a miner makes a serious force attack? Now Casper's finalized blockchain can prevent PoW attackers, even if 51% or more of the computing power trying to rewrite the history other than the latest checkpoint will be blocked. So Casper provides security. Unlike CTFG, because CFFG is a layer of coverage on different proposed mechanisms, Casper cannot ensure activity because activity is dependent on the proposed mechanism.

The verifiers are motivated to assemble on the chain of authority because they will be punished if they continue to vote on different chains. The formation of slasher 2.0 allows the verifier to be punished not only for double voting but also for voting on the incorrect chain. However, this also creates a dilemma, where the verifier is worried that if there is a branch and he is not sure which one is authoritative, and if he voted on the incorrect chain, he chooses to cut off or to leave the voting.

Clear features of CFFG:

■ Finalization: Finalization over 20 minutes. Finalize the block every 50 blocks (one cycle) to prevent PoW mining brute force attack
■ Consensus security
■ Proven activity
■ Priority availability.

(3) CTFG

CTFG is a correct construction (CBC) consensus agreement designed to combat the real environment of oligopoly. CTFG is a PoS adaptation of the GHOS or GHOST protocol in the proof of workload for its fork selection rules. The guiding design principles behind CTFG are based on cryptographic economics with formal methods designed to achieve security. Unlike the CFFG hybrid protocol detailed above, CTFG is a purely PoS.

> Casper was born as simply "the friendly ghost", an adaptation of GHOST to proof-of-stake, complete with incentives that would make a cartel "friendly" to non-cartel validators.
>
> *Vlad Zamfir, Chapter 5 of Casper's History*

Similar to the proof of workload, CTFG trades off consistency and usability. In particular, when the blocks are not finalized, they will be safer as the depth deeper in the chain. CTFG is a bit like CFFG, and the processing of the chain header is always much faster than the finalization of the block.

The biggest difference between Casper's PoS proposal mechanism and the Tendermint proposal mechanism is that compared to the pseudo-random selection leader, the former's verifier can propose blocks based on the blocks they see.

Casper provides a unique feature which is the parameter-ized safety margin. Similar to using six acknowledgments in Bitcoin to determine an economic final state, "evaluation security" in CTFG, a verifier can have a different security threshold function than other verifiers. Casper is designed to allow verifiers to choose their own fault-tolerant thresh-olds while maintaining low PoS overhead in the network.

Casper's core advantage over Tendermint is that the network can accommodate a certain number of validators at any time. Block confirmation time should be shorter because the blocks in Tendermint need to be finalized when they are created. In order to achieve short block times, there needs to be a limit on the number of validators that Tendermint PoS can accommodate. Since CTFG and CFFG do not need security when the block is created, the Ethereum network, in comparison to cosmoses'100 validators, can accommodate a larger number of validators.

Clear features of CTFG

- Availability. Casper's nodes can be divided before they reach a consensus.
- Asynchronous security.
- Survival. Casper's decision can survive partial synchronization, but not survive in asynchronous.
- Cartel resistance. Casper is built on the basis of boycotting oligopolistic attackers, so certifiers can go beyond the agreement without any collusion.
- Security, depending on the evaluator's assessment security threshold.

3.2.3 Trap of Proof-of-Stake

(1) Relations with No Interest

At first, there were many different ways to describe the general trap of PoS, and "relations with no interest" was raised at this time. Jae Kwon first mentioned this issue in May 2014 with the unfortunate name of "Bad Choice Paradox". In July 2014, Vitalik popularized the problem of the exact definitions described by Bitcoin developers as relations with "no interest".

The problem is following: at a given block height, the verifier can effectively compromise security by voting for multiple conflicting blocks without paying any price for it.

A simple PoS design is very vulnerable to these attacks. It is a disaster, because there is no incentive to encourage everyone to focus on a single chain all the time, and each incentive is to be repeatedly signed on multiple conflicting chains at once, in order to get more block incentives. Economically optimal strategy becomes as much as possible to vote on multiple forks, as shown in Figure 3.4.

In the proof of workload, for miners who are mining on multiple chains, if they want to do harm, they must separate their very scarce computing resources and use this high cost to curb the evil situation. In modern nondegenerate PoS, this cost is designed into the agreement to

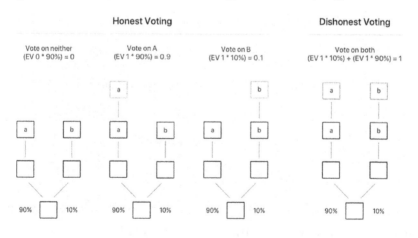

Figure 3.4 Honest Voting vs. Dishonest Voting in PoS. https://www.bcskill.com/index.php/archives/793.html

mimic the limitations of PoW physical mining for miners. For example, Ethereum leader Vitalik Buterin introduced the "slasher" concept in January 2014, and the penalty within the agreement can mitigate this attack.

In the same year, Jae Kwon further promoted this method, which is the first iteration to implement the Tendermint consensus protocol. Increasing costs and allowing harsh penalties were helpful for all non-degenerate BFT protocols, and even the three consensuses presented in this section are used.

(2) Remote Attack

Since the user has the right to withdraw the deposit in the PoS mechanism, there is a hidden danger of remote attack. That's because an attacker can fork over any block length without worrying about being cut. Because once the margin is unbound, the incentive to not vote long distances from a block height is canceled. In other words, when more than 2/3 of the certifiers unbind, they can maliciously create a second chain containing the previous set of certifiers, which could result in arbitrary transactions.

This is quite fatal for the PoS protocol because the security model for PoS must be "subjective". (what is a "subjective" security model? If the information can be verified within the agreement, it can be called "objective"; if the information must be verified by means other than the protocol, it is called "subjective".) After a new node joins the network, it may draw different conclusions about the state of the current network. Because their decisions are based on subjective information, that is, social reputation. At this point, however, we compare it with the PoW and find that the security model of the PoW must be "objective" because their decisions are based on objective information and the current network state is always in the situation of with the highest workload, and the new node always has the same conclusion about the network state.

So how to prevent the harm of long-range attacks?

Under the weak subjective model proposed by Vitalik, while accessing a new node in the network for verification, the current node must be bound to the deposit. Only if the verification node has paid a deposit, his signature is economically meaningful. This means that the client can only rely on the signature of the verification node that has locked deposit. Therefore, when the client receives and authenticates the consensus data, the chain of consensus approval must come from the block of the verification node that currently locked the deposit. In comparison with the PoW protocol, the consensus-recognized chain is derived from the Genesis block – as long as you know the data of the Genesis block, you can identify the chain of consensus recognition. Here, as long as you know the verification node that currently locks the deposit, you can identify the chain of consensus approval. A client that does not know the list of authentication nodes that currently locked the deposit must obtain this list through another channel first. This restriction identifies the consensus by asking everyone to use current information.

In addition, the process of unbinding deposit must go through a "thaw" period. Unbinding can cause delays in message synchronization for weeks to months, requiring time to "thaw". Because the agreement forbids to recover before the Nth block, where N is the length of the deposit, this rule invalidates any long-range forks. At the same time, synchronizing data requires obtaining the character of the latest locked deposit verification node list from other channels, which achieves the "weak subjectivity" as Vitalik says.

Casper(s) and Tendermint use this simple locking mechanism (commonly known as "freeze" in "Tendermint") to lock the equity for a period of time ("thaw" from weeks to months) in case any verification node maliciously compromises system security. In CFFG algorithm research, led by Vitalik Buterin, the fork can only modify the block after the final block, thus preventing remote attacks. In CFFG, attempts to modify such long-distance bifurcations of blocks earlier than the final block by using timestamps are not recognized by the protocol.

(3) Cartel Formation

PoS still has a problem to solve, that is, the problem of oligopoly, and of course, this is also the problem that any economic form needs to face.

> Cryptocurrency is incredibly concentrated. So is mining power. Oligopolistic competition is the norm in many "real-life" markets. Coordination between a small number of relatively wealthy validators is much

easier than coordination between a large number of relatively poor validators. Cartels formation is completely expected, in our context.

Vlad Zamfir, Chapter 4 of "The History of Casper"

Tendermint relies on additional protocol management methods to confront oligopoly verifiers. Although there is no agreement on the censorship system, relying on out-of-band social information to solve the problem of the cartel formation, the basic principle is that the user will inevitably notice the formation of the cartel, and the society will also gossip about it. Then, give up or vote to reorganize the blocked blockchain.

So far, Vlad's Casper protocol is the only one that explicitly uses consensus within the review incentives to combat a cartel formation.

(4) Future Work

The operation of the public chain on the product is still a relatively new technology. The only security model that has so far shown to be non-corrupt is the proof of workload. The design space for the proof of equity is still very large, and the engineering understanding is not enough, because the proof of equity is a cutting-edge research field, and there is still not enough data support at the present days. To achieve an optimal PoS consensus algorithm, we still have a lot of future work to do.

The first direction in which the future can work is probably Tendermint. It might be to propose a new improvement mechanism for it, or to compress Tendermint's multiple rounds of voting into one round of voting.

The second area of future work may be to use a more advanced encryption technique to make the signature of the block header smaller. Because we are building a "blockchain internet" through Cosmos, moving our client certification from one chain to another is our core job. From this point of view, it is very advantageous to use a more advanced cryptography to reduce the size of the block header by thirty times or more.

In addition, we can optimize the p2p layer so that we can significantly reduce the amount of traffic required by the final block. In the future work, not only the amount of data in the header of the compressed block, but also the amount of data sent to the peer could be reduced. In this case, a larger set of verifiers can be added above the threshold of the initial 100 verifiers of the Cosmos network.

3.3 PBFT Optimized Version: Federal Byzantine Agreement (FBA)

In the traditional PBFT, the Byzantine Agreement can guarantee the achievement of distributed consensus despite the spoilers that lead to Byzantine mistakes. However, it requires all participants of the system to agree, and all nodes in the network must be known and pre-authenticated.

Anyone of the Federal Byzantine Agreements (FBAs) can join, distributed way group (quorum or nodes are sufficient) can come to a compromise, each node can determine its trustworthy object, and different nodes do not need to trust the same participant combination in order to complete the consensus. Flexible trust means that users are free to trust any combination of participants who believe that they are appropriate.

The Stellar Consensus Protocol (SCP), proposed by Stellar.org's chief scientific officer, Professor David Mazières, is the first example of a Federated Byzantine Agreement (FBA). The Stellar Consensus Agreement provides a way to reach a consensus by accurately recording financial transactions without relying on closed systems. The Stellar Consensus Agreement also has four key attributes: decentralized control, low latency, flexible trust, and asymptotic security. As a FBA, the Stellar Consensus Agreement increases tolerance for irrational behavior, requiring only limited computing resources and reducing barriers to entry.

Before we explain the FBA in detail, we need to know what is the legal unit?

In a distributed system, a legal unit is a collection of nodes that meet the reached agreement. The FBA introduces the concept of a quorum, a subset of statutes that can persuade a particular node to agree.

FBA's main features:

Each node in the FBA can select its own legal unit sets, and the quorum results of the entire system are determined by the choices made by a single node. This is

the key difference between the Byzantine (BA) protocol system and the FBA system.

In FBA, there are no goalkeepers, no centralists, and
individual nodes can decide which participants they
should trust. Nodes can choose multiple groups, and
the choice of individual nodes may depend on standards outside the system. For example, if a bank is
considered to have a good reputation, then all transactions on other nodes require its approval.

There are different states in the relationship between legal
units:

■ Legal unit with intersection: good legal units share
their nodes, causing node overlap between different
legal units.
■ Legal unit with no intersection: when there is no
intersection between units, we get legal unit with no
intersection.

If the corpus does not intersect, for example, Statute A
approved a statement of a pizza order, and Statute B
approved a statement of a hamburger order. Because they
can independently recognize contradictory statements, cor-
puses without intersection could be harmful for consensus.

So how do you get the nodes to make better choices?

Each node in the FBA system is responsible for ensuring that the selected legal unit does not violate the legal
body intersection. It is often necessary to confirm whether
the quorum cluster is large enough and whether the

nodes contained in the cluster are important enough to not deceive or generate different information for different people and endanger their own reputation.

Federal vote: accept, confirm.

Nodes in the FBA system use a federated voting technique to implement their protocols. Federal voting techniques are used to guide the FBA system or a group of people working together to reach an agreement. In Stellar's white paper, it is given the following example:

Lunch consensus

To describe in details the process of voting for a node and ultimately accepting a statement while allowing the system to agree, let us give an example that many people are familiar with. Let's talk about a group of people voting for what to eat for lunch. In this case, the name of the person is the node, and all food options are the declarations that the node needs to refer to.

Vanessa works in a public office, where a large group of people are booking lunch according to their wishes. There are a lot of options, and not everyone will make a choice; when it is determined that there are enough people, they will place an order.

Vanessa and his work colleagues decided to use the FBA-based SCP to deal with this problem.

Initial vote

We assume that Vanessa wants pizza, but still needs to be open-minded, in case the majority of people in this group choose other options apart from pizza.

Voting is a preparation for work and happens only in the node phase. In the first step of the federal election process, Vanessa stated that the pizza was valid and promised that if there won't be any, she would not vote for any option apart from pizza. Unless enough of her work companions voted for the pizza, she might get the result of accepting a non-pizza option.

Acception (Admittance)

Fortunately, there is a legal body intersection, and the body group can affect other nodes. Imagine another situation where Vanessa voted for hamburger. But remember, voting is just a preparation.

Winnie, Andrew, and Eva are all in the legal unit with Vanessa, and they can stop the process of accepting burgers. A v-blocking (v-shaped) set of nodes contains at least one node from all of Vanessa's body groups and blocks all behaviors in the statute containing Vanessa, causing Vanessa to accept pizza.

In the following situations, Vanessa actually accepted the pizza:

She has never accepted a statement that contradicts pizza.

Members of each v-shaped restricted set declare to accept pizza, or each collective member that includes Vanessa also votes for pizza or declares to accept pizza.

Official approval

When every quorum member votes for pizza, we say that this statute recognizes pizza. A node does not need to recognize the statement personally.

For example, Scott often relies on Andrew and Iris to decide what to eat. They are the legal unit of Scott. If all three of them voted for pizza, the unit approved the pizza.

A working companion can vote for a lunch option and then accept a lunch that is different from his vote. Vote pizza doesn't have to insist on pizza for lunch – pizza is accepted as lunch only when it is approved.

Confirmation

Confirmation is a final step in the electoral process, and it will result in a consistent agreement across the system. To ensure consensus, the nodes exchange confirmation messages with each other. The system agrees to a statement; once sufficient messages are distributed and processed, regardless of what happens afterwards, each active, error-free node will accept the statement.

For example, Eva declares that she accepts pizza and sends a confirmation message, "accept(pizza)", which is shorthand for "I have accepted pizza".

When Eva sends a confirmation message, Winnie, Andrew, Graydon, and others in the Eva statute broadcast "accept(pizza)".

These messages can convince another person to accept the pizza. In the above example, if Vanessa voted against the pizza, for example, if the v-type limit set accepts the pizza, then Vanessa accepts the pizza. These other people convince more people as much as possible, always broadcasting "accept(pizza)" until everyone can accept the pizza.

Subsequent confirmation of the statute of the message allows Vanessa to confirm the pizza and achieve a system agreement. The company ordered pizza, and everyone was happy.

This example fully illustrates the entire process of FBA system implementation.

3.4 Other: Algorand Agreement

Turing Award winner and MIT professor Sivio Micali designed the Algorand Consensus Agreement, a new encryption consensus mechanism that validates transactions in a very short time and extends to many users. Algorand ensures that users never disagree on confirmed transactions, even if some users are malicious, the network is temporarily partitioned. In contrast, the existing cryptocurrency allows for temporary forks, so it takes a long time, about an hour, and finally the number of acknowledgments is used to ensure that the transaction is confirmed.

Algorand uses the new BA protocol agreement to reach user consensus in the next set of transactions. To extend the consensus to many users, Algorand uses a new mechanism based on verifiable random functions that allows users to self-check whether they are selected to participate in the BA protocol to license the next set of transactions. In Algorand's BA protocol, in addition to the private key, the user does not retain any private state, allowing

Algorand to replace the participant immediately after sending the message. This can mitigate targeted attacks on selected participants after their identity is revealed.

In Algorand, users reached a consensus on the new block through BA. The BA is very fast to execute. Generally speaking, the BA has three substeps per cycle, and each time there is more than 1/3 probability to reach a consensus. Once the "verifier" has reached a consensus on a new block, more than half of the "verifiers" will electronically sign the block with their own private key (equivalent to authentication), and the block will begin to spread in the Algorand network. An important feature of BA is that BA participants can be replaced (player-replaceable) in a peer-to-peer network communication. That is, each substep of each cycle of the BA can be performed by a new, independently randomly selected participant. In this case, BA can still reach a consensus correctly and effectively. Assuming there are millions of users, the participants in each substep of the BA can be completely different, and each batch of participants cannot determine who is the next group of participants and thus cannot collude.

According to Algorand's team test, we can evaluate Algorand's performance on 1000 EC2 virtual machines, simulating up to 500,000 users. The experimental results show that Algorand confirms the transaction within one minute, achieves 125 times the throughput of Bitcoin, hardly expands for more users, and almost does not cause fines for more users, but Algorand has a big problem that there is no incentive mechanism, so running in a completely decentralized environment requires practical tests.

Chapter 4

Game Theory and Cryptoeconomics

4.1 What Is Game Theory?

Game theory is an analysis toolkit which is designed to help us to understand the observed phenomena of interactions between decision-making bodies. Basic assumption implied by this theory is that decision-makers pursue determined external goals (they are rational) and consider their own knowledge or the expectations of other decision-making actors (their reasoning is strategic).

Game theory has a long history, for example, "The Art of War" in ancient China. At the very beginning, game theory was researching questions of losing and winning in playing chess, bridge, gambling, it was mainly based on practical experience, it wasn't developing theoretically, so officially, it was developed into a discipline only at the beginning of the 20th century.

The study of game theory began with Zermelo, Borel and von Neumann, and von Neumann and Oskar Morgenstern was systematized and formalized for the first time. Then, John Forbes Nash Jr. used the fixed-point theorem to prove the existence of equilibrium points, which laid a solid foundation for the generalization of game theory.

From an economical point of view, everyone thinks that modern economic game theory was introduced in the 1950s by famous American mathematician von Neumann and an economist Oscar Morgenstern. It has become one of the main tools of economic analysis and has made very important contributions to the development of economic theory such as industrial organization theory, principal-agent theory, and information economics. The Nobel Prize in Economics in 1994 and 1996 was given to economists who have been studying game theory.

Game theory considers the predictive behavior and actual behavior of individuals in a group environment with specific rules. There are three basic elements: Players, Strategies, and Payoffs. Game theory assumes the following:

■ Participants are rational and maximize their own interests.
■ Participants form correct beliefs and expectations about the environment and the behavior of other participants in the environment.

That means, in a strategy combination, all participants will encounter a following situation: when the other person does not change the strategy, his strategy at this time is the best – this is the famous Nash equilibrium. At the Nash equilibrium point, every rational participant does not have the impulse to change the strategy alone. At this time, if he changes the strategy, his interests will decrease.

The classification of the game also has different classifications according to different benchmarks. It is generally believed that games can be mainly divided into cooperative games and non-cooperative games. The difference between a cooperative game and a non-cooperative game is whether there is a binding agreement between the parties that interact with each other. If there is, it is a cooperative game. If not, it is a non-cooperative game.

From the time series of behavior, game theory is further divided into two categories: static game and dynamic game. Static game means that in the game, the participants choose at the same time or even if it is not at the same time, the actors do not know what specific actions have been taken. Dynamic game means that in the game, the actions of the participants are in order, and then actors can observe the actions selected by the first actors. Simply it could be understood as "prisoner's dilemma", which means a simultaneous decision, which belongs to the static game; and the decision-making games such as chess or games where the actions have the priority of order belong to the dynamic game.

According to the degree of understanding of the participants to other participants, they are divided into a complete information game and an incomplete information game. Full game means that in the process of game, each participant has accurate information about the characteristics, strategy space, and income function of other participants; incomplete information game refers to the game where characteristics, strategic space, and the income function information of the participants are not accurate enough or accurate for not all of the participants.

4.2 Nash Equilibrium

Let's return to the classic prisoner's dilemma question and explain Nash equilibrium, the quintessence of game theory, and cryptoeconomics:

Suppose there are two participants and a banker. Each participant has two cards: each with "cooperation" and "betrayal". Participants each placed a card face down and placed it in front of the dealer. That excludes the possibility of participants knowing the choice of the other party. The dealer then opens the cards of two participants and pays the proceeds of both parties according to the following rules:

■ One person betrayed, one person cooperated: the traitor got five points (interest drive) and the collaborator zero points (payment fraud).
■ Both of them cooperate: each got three points (cooperative compensation).
■ Both of them betrayed: each got one point (betrayal punishment).

The matrix of interest's decision is the following:

	Participants 2 Cooperator	Participant 2 Betrayer
Participant 1 Cooperator	3, 3	0, 5
Participant 1 Betrayer	5, 0	1, 1

But there is a problem in this. If there is an environment like blockchain that has no trust foundation (such as the forked income is greater than the mining in the original chain), the benefits of betrayer participants 1 and 2 are greater than the cooperators, so what's the solution? For example, there is a following matrix of interest's decision:

	Participant 2 Cooperator	Participant 2 Betrayer
Participant 1 Cooperator	3, 3	0, 5
Participant 1 Betrayer	5, 0	6, 6

In the blockchain, it is possible that the participants will completely ignore interests of all for the benefit of the individual. At this time, the "punishment" mechanism is particularly important. If we can set a mechanism as following: all betraying actions (unfavorable to the overall interest) are punished with six additional points, and the new matrix of interests' decision becomes like this:

	Participant 2 Cooperator	Participant 2 Betrayer
Participant 1 Cooperator	3, 3	0, −1
Participant 1 Betrayer	−1, 0	0, 0

We can see that after joining the punishment mechanism, the Nash equilibrium has changed from being a betrayal (conduct malicious behavior) to cooperating. This mechanism is a very important part of the economic model of the blockchain.

4.3 Schelling Point

Schelling point is the tendency of people in game theory to choose without communication. This choice may be because it looks natural, special, or related to the selector. This concept was coined by Thomas Schelling, a Nobel laureate in the United States, in the 1960s in the book *The Strategy of Conflict*. On page 57, Schelling describes "Some focal point for each person's expectation of what the other expects him to expect to be expected to do".[1] This concept was later named after Schelling.

---

[1] T. Schelling: *The Strategy of Conflict*, Harvard University Press, Cambridge, MA, 1980, p. 57.

For example, a group of independent and non-communicating people are required to select a number from the following figures, and only when the same number is selected by all of them, there will be a reward:

38219057301490231
100000000000
1.43123289.

They may choose the number 100000000000 at the same time, because it looks the most natural, and it is also the number that everyone expects others to choose. The other two numbers have no significant features.

4.4 Bounded Rationality Model

Another concept in game theory that is crucial to crypto-economics is bounded rationality model. After the 1950s, it was recognized that an economy based on completely rational decision-making theory was only an ideal model, and it was impossible to guide actual decision-making. Herbent Simon proposed satisfaction criteria and bounded rationality model criteria, to replace the "economic man" with "social people". The bounded rational model is also known as Simon's model and Simon's bounded rationality model. This is a more realistic model, which believes that human reason is a bounded rationality between perfect rationality and total irrationality.

Bounded rationality model believes that decision-makers pursue rationality, but it is not the pursuit of rationality to the maximum. He only requires bounded rationality. This is because people's knowledge, ability, or time is limited, and decision-makers can neither grasp all the information nor understand the detailed rules of decision-making. At the same time, the bounded rationality model believes that decision-makers pursue "satisfaction" standards rather than optimal standards in decision-making.

Let's take an example. Xiao Li every time uses his card to enter the gym. Once he was using his card to enter the gym, he found out that there is no one at the front desk and there are 5 yuan on the table. The limited rational model thinks that Xiao Li will not take these 5 yuan, because not take is against Xiao Li's habits, the simplest decision, taking 5 yuan may impact Xiao Li's daily fitness more, so Xiao Li will make not to take 5-yuan decision under limited conditions. This concept is very important for the design of harmful mechanism in cryptoeconomics.

4.5 Game Theory Mechanism Design and Consensus Mechanism

The design of the consensus mechanism on the blockchain is most similar to the design of the game theory mechanism. The mechanism design is often called reverse game theory, because we start from a desired result and reverse derivative to design a complete game. If the players pursue their own interests in the game, it will produce the results that we want. For example, imagine that we are responsible for designing an auction rule, and our goal is to expect bidders to win the bid for the actual value of a product. To achieve this goal, we use game theory to design the auction into a game in which each player's core strategy is to be able to bid on real value.

The consensus mechanism design focuses on the system design and system establishment as game theory mechanism design does. As in our auction example, we use game theory to design a set of rules or mechanisms that can produce a custom balance. In the design of consensus mechanisms, we use cryptography and computer programming to implement this economic incentive. We design the systems that are usually distributed and decentralized.

Bitcoin's consensus algorithm Proof of Work (PoW) is the result of this approach. Nakamoto wanted Bitcoin to have certain characteristics, such as its ability to reach a consensus on its internal state and its ability to resist censorship. He then designed an entire Bitcoin system to implement these characteristics, assuming that people responded to economic incentives in a reasonable way.

4.6 Game Theory Mechanism Design and Blockchain Security

In the real world of business, a hostile takeover is a behavior that greatly affects the security of the company. A malicious acquirer usually does not have the consent of the other party and wants to obtain control and all resources which has the other party. In the world of blockchains, there are similar security risks, and it is called the bribing attacker model.

The bribery attacker model refers to an uncoordinated choice model, such as the Trustless Blockchain, where there is a briber with sufficient resources, who is using an additional economic reward (Bribery) to motivate other participants to take specific actions. The specific actions here usually have a greater impact on the security of the original blockchain system. For example, the most common is the malicious fork.

If we use a malicious acquisition to analogize the bribery attacker model, we can explain that a briber outside a blockchain agreement acquires tokens or mining power through a condition, thereby achieving the purpose of attacking the original blockchain. In layman's terms, it is called "buy existing nodes".

In order to better understand how the briber achieves its purpose, we use the popular game theory knowledge to make an analysis.

Let's assume that there is a simple voting mechanism, each participant in the blockchain can vote for both 0 and 1. The assumption that 0 is beneficial to the original blockchain, and 1 is unfavorable to the original blockchain. Only when the results of everyone's vote are the same, everyone can get the corresponding reward P. In this case, the Nash equilibrium is that everyone voted 0, that is, the decision that is favorable to the original blockchain, and the profit matrix of decision is expressed as follows:

	You vote 0	You vote 1
The other people vote 0	P, P	0, 0
The other people vote1	0, 0	P, P

If there is a bribery attacker at this time, he tells you that if you vote for 1 while others don't vote for 1, there is an additional reward ε in addition to the reward P, and then a new profit matrix of decision looks like this:

	You vote 0	You vote1
The other people vote 0	P, P	0, P + ε
The other people vote 1	0, 0	P, P

On the surface, it is the best choice for you to vote. The problem is that when the briber tells everyone the bribe conditions, everyone thinks that vote 1 is the best choice, and then the Nash equilibrium at this time becomes everyone's vote; that is, everyone has chosen the decision, which is unfavorable for original blockchain.

The briber achieved his goal through this P + ε attack and at the same time did not have to pay the promised bribe ε to make decisions that were unfavorable to the original blockchain. Very smart and clever, isn't it? This P + ε attack problem is also one of the security risks similar to the PoW consensus mechanism.

One solution is to introduce an improved PoS consensus mechanism with margin and penalties. Since each blockchain participant has a margin on the chain, if the bribe comes in and tells you to make a decision that is unfavorable to the original blockchain, you will lose all your margin and you will feel that it is not worth the effort. What's more, in the above decision-making payoff matrix, we also know that even if you make a decision that is unfavorable to the original blockchain, you can't get the extra compensation ε promised by the briber, no matter how big the ε is.

4.7 Prospect of Game Theory-Based Consensus Mechanism – Ethereum's Casper Consensus Algorithm

Casper is an optimized version of PoS consensus mechanism for Ethereum to transform from PoW to PoS. Ethereum's core contributor Vitalik Buterin intends to use Casper for permanent divergence of Ethereum to achieve this transformation. In general, Casper requires validators to place a majority of the margin on the consensus outcome. The consensus result is formed by the certifier's betting situation: the certifier must guess which other person will bet on which block to win, and also bet the block. If the bet is correct, they can get back the margin plus the transaction fee, and maybe there will be some new currency; if the bet does not reach a quick agreement, they can only get back some of the margin. Therefore, the certifier's bet distribution will converge after several rounds. In addition, if the verifier changes the bet too significantly, such as first betting that a block has a high probability of winning, and then betting that another block has a high probability of winning, he will be severely punished. This rule ensures that the verifier only bets with a high probability if he is very convinced that other people also believe that a block has a high probability of winning. Casper uses this mechanism to ensure that no bets converge on one result and then converge to another, as long as the certifier is sufficient. The verifier places a bet on each candidate block at each height h, assigns each block a winning probability, and publishes it. By repeatedly betting, the certifier will select a unique winning block for each height h, and this process also determines the order in which the trades are executed. If a verifier publishes a probability distribution greater than 100% at a certain height, or publishes a probability of less than 0%, or assigns a probability of greater than 0% to an invalid block, Casper will punish his margin.

In short, the Casper Equity Proof attempts to provide a very large security margin for cryptoeconomics, by enforcing a large Ethereum security deposit instead of computer computing, which implements the certifier's functionality. This security deposit, or cryptoeconomy proof, proved to be a powerful deterrent. The idea is clear at a glance – if you create the trouble on the blockchain, you will lose everything.

Casper forces participants to join a Schelling Coin game. Participants were forced to place their security deposits on what most people would bet. Using the same recursive logic, most participants will accurately vote for a valid transaction because each participant expects others to reach the same conclusion. This is the case, when the proof of equity can resist the $P + \varepsilon$ attack, because in the event that they will eventually vote for the minority, the attacker will have to provide a very large budget to subsidize the participant's security deposit.

In the context of these security models, we can see that Casper's resilience is concentrated in the uncoordinated selection model and stems from bribery attackers. Casper is also theoretically sensitive to 51% of attacks originating from cooperate attacker models. But, like Bitcoin, Ethereum has raised the cost of making such an attack to such a high level that it has almost completely contained it. In the Casper environment, the threat of losing all relevant rights is even a stronger shock.

Chapter 5

Behavioral Economics and Cryptoeconomics

5.1 Behavioral Economics vs. Traditional Economics: Irrational vs. Rational

Traditional economics assumes that people are rational – the implication of this assumption is that we can calculate and scale the value of all the choices we face in our daily lives and choose the one that is most beneficial to us. And once we make mistakes and do irrational things, through the "power of the market" will quickly pull us back to the path of correct rationality. Based on these assumptions, from Adam Smith, generations of economists have derived far-reaching and all-encompassing conclusions: from taxation to health policy to the pricing of goods and services.

However, we are far less rational than the traditional economic theory assumes. We often do things that are impulsive and even not in our own interests (such as we know that staying up late is bad for the body, but still looking around). Not only that, but our irrational behaviors are not irregular and unconscious, but systematic and even predictable, and this is the goal pursued by behavioral economics.

Behavioral economics uses the knowledge of social psychology to study the influence of information activities on the economic activities. It starts from people's actual behaviors and helps us to understand the various anomalies hidden in daily life correctly.

This chapter does not cover any complex and unfamiliar concepts or principles, but rather comes from the practical scenarios that everyone is familiar with, discussing the shortcomings of our usual behavioral decisions, and what behavioral economics and cryptographic economics can help us with.

5.2 Behavioral Economics in the Blockchain World

5.2.1 How to Introduce Blockchain to Friends?

> "What is a blockchain?"
> "What is Bitcoin?"

All people in the industry will be asked the above questions while introducing the blockchain to friends. Can you answer it in a concise and clear sentence?

> Blockchain is a new application model for computer technologies such as distributed data storage, point-to-point transmission, consensus mechanisms, and encryption algorithms.
> Bitcoin is a decentralized, point-to-point form of encrypted digital currency system.

If you originally answer in accordance with Baidu Encyclopedia's introduction (it takes time for you to memorize them precisely), the other party's great probability is incomprehensible, because it is difficult to intuitively understand the meaning of these two sentences, so you can simply explain as following:

> The blockchain is the next generation of the Internet. Before we could only send information through the network, now we can pass the value directly.
> The current transfer is made through Bank, Alipay or WeChat; if Bitcoin is used, we can transfer directly without any third party.

By comparing the blockchain with the Internet, Bitcoin, and the bank, even if the other party can't fully understand the specific details, it can form a more direct and specific impression in the mind, because the objects of comparison are things we know well.

Behavioral psychology points out that there is no "internal value meter" in our hearts to tell us what the true value of an item is; instead, we are concerned with the relative merits of this item and other items to estimate its value. For example, even if you don't know the price of the ant S9 miner, you can infer that it is more expensive than the S10.

In cryptoeconomics, value is often determined by comparison: how to ensure the fairness of miners who are mining in systems such as Bitcoin and Ethereum? We can compare the speed of solving the problems, who can solve the problems quicker, and who can get the right to add the transaction to the public ledger; for various consensus mechanisms, such as PoW, PoS, and DPoS, we have been comparing which one represents the future direction more.

Our comparative habit is not only irrational, but this irrationality is predictable. We always rely on observing the things around us to determine each other's relationships, not only in tangible objects, but also in intangible experiences, even when we are dealing with temporarily volatile things such as feelings, attitudes, and opinions.

Relativity helps us make decisions in our lives, but it can also make us feel very painful. For example, your normal annual salary before contacting the blockchain is 100K RMB, and it becomes 500K RMB after investing in Bitcoin. This is of course a happy thing; but if you know that the friends around you earn at least 100,000K RMB, can you still be happy?

If we can control the scope of our comparison and turn to a circle that can improve our relative happiness, we will live a more comfortable life.

5.2.2 *Why Are You Completely Indifferent to $10,000 Bitcoin, While Some People Are Crazy for it?*

Starting from late 2017, countries began to control initial coin offering (ICO). The cryptocurrency was falling all the time, and price cut half was only basic. Eighty percent fall was also everywhere, causing countless people to suffer heavy losses.

However, after 3 months of market regulation, the cryptocurrency market has turned into a big bull market. Numerous currencies that were considered lingering on in a steadily worsening condition have been revived, and the second spring was more dazzling than before. Bitcoin broke through the price of 14K RMB in December, and let countless people sigh and miss the best speculative opportunities.

Some people fled in any path they could without considering during this period, and the others were calmly buying bottomed out tokens; why did different people made a different choice in the face of the same situation?

Behavioral economics points out that when people make decisions, thinking is often influenced by the first information they get, just like the anchor that sinks into the sea, fixing your mind somewhere, and then you are not aware of yourself. The impact of this is called the "anchoring effect".

The anchoring effect is a good explanation for our different acceptance of bitcoin prices, and the different people have significantly different understanding of the value, when they have a contact with bitcoin and try to understand bitcoin for the first time:

A thinks that Bitcoin is a string of useless code. It doesn't have the attributes of money at all. Now the price is due to hype. Sooner or later, there will be a bubble bursting day. They are not ready to accept that the price was rising all over its history, and definitely won't buy it, for example, such as Professor Lang, who is famous for rejecting 100 bitcoins.

B believes that bitcoin is produced by mining, so its price should be equal to the cost of mining bitcoin (equipment input + electricity fee + repair), so it will be sold above cost, such as 10K bitcoin for two Papa John's Pizzas.

C believes that Bitcoin is one of the future global payment methods, which can match the current total value of gold, so each bitcoin is worth about $1,300.

D believes that Bitcoin will completely subvert the existing financial system, equal to the total global value of the future, so the current price is still low in the long run, just like it is often said: "Now it is the best time than ever to buy bottomed out tokens for the long run".

We don't need to evaluate the rationality of the above ideas, but simply analyze the first impressions of different people on the value of Bitcoin during the first contact.

Unless there is any major event which can subvert the cognition, then the initial value/price in the future will be used as an "anchor point" to become an important criterion for judging whether it should be bought/sold at present.

The same reason can also be used in the ICO. When the whole coin economy grows wildly in 2017, projects with cryptoinfluencers listed as consultants in the whitepaper tend to grasp more attention and get more funding, as for people who don't understand the project basics, such "anchoring" consultants influence people's judgements.

The above illustrates that in the decisions we make, whether inadvertent or well thought out, "anchoring" plays a great role.

The cryptocurrency market can be seen as a complete free market: if you think a project is promising, then you invest and such an exchange is beneficial to both parties. In other words, whether the exchange behavior is mutually beneficial depends on whether the parties in the market are really clear about the value of the exchanged items.

However, if our choices are often influenced by our initial "anchor", the choices made on this may not accurately reflect the practical value and pleasure we get from this project (whether many items are really useful or it is still unknown). In this way, if we can't accurately calculate the value of the project and just blindly follow the cryptoinfluencers, we can't figure out if the deal will benefit us.

For example, due to the unfortunate initial anchor, we may mistakenly use Bitcoin (the initial anchor price is lower) to invest some junk projects (the initial anchor pricing could be on the contrary, higher), and in the end, we are finished.

Perhaps it's time to check out the "anchor" in the currency circle we are staying. Was it a big coffee that we've been praising before, or do you still want to be as reliable as you thought? Have you ever sworn that you won't sell and still decided to leave in your hands after re-examining the project? Once we rethink the old choices, we will open our doors to new decisions, new days, and new opportunities.

And when we rethink our previous "anchor", the blockchain can help us to a large extent. Because of its irreversible nature of information records, we can look up all the records and have one of them. The performance of the series is re-evaluated – history is always the best teacher.

5.2.3 Why Do So Many Projects Like Airdrops?

One day you got home from work, and while you were lying on the sofa and habitually opened the imToken wallet, and then found a strange token in the balance list and a number of tokens. If you are just starting to encounter this situation, I believe you will be at least a little bit excited, but now you got used to it: it is just some project's "airdrop".

"Airdrop" refers to a large amount of tokens (also called "free candy") that a certain person or an organization will send to the user's wallet. Many users will not refuse this and will even take the initiative to find various channels of information to get free candies; there are also people who have designed the corresponding programs and websites to collect information about the latest project airdrops.

In addition to airdrops, there is a mainstream way to get the project tokens for free, and it often appears in various WeChat groups for speculators or circle of friends.

This is not only the promotion of the project itself, but also many exchanges obtain users in this way (such as free delivery of their own platform tokens), especially good effect is when it is especially effective when exchanges reward a user based on how many people he invites.

It's no secret that free things make people feel good. "Zero" is not just a special way of expressing prices, but can also evoke passionate emotions – a source of irrational excitement. If the unit price of a project's token is reduced from 1 RMB to 5 JIAO, will you participate? Possibly yes. If it is changed from 5 JIAO to free? Will you fight to reach for it? Definitely will!

Zero cost is so irresistible, what is going on? Why this thing makes us so happy? After all, free is likely to cause troubles for us: what we didn't intend to buy, or who didn't ever want to buy, would become incredibly attractive as soon as it becomes free.

Have you registered an exchange that you have never heard in order to get a free token and have real-name certification?

The biggest problem of free tokens is that it lures you to struggle between it and another project – and leads you to make unwise decisions. If you think that the blockchain + Internet of Things has great potential for development, you want to invest in projects in this field. After you have read the white paper of a project, you feel that your team and technology are OK, but you have invested another one that looks a little bit worse than the previous one because it has an extra 30% discount. You give up a better choice and invest in a project that you didn't want, which is a great deal!

Why is it so tempting in the end? Why do we have an irrational impulse to get free things, even if you don't really need them?

Adam Ereli, an economist at the Massachusetts Institute of Technology, believes the majority of transactions have both positive and negative aspects, but freedom makes us forget the negative ones. Free tokens create an emotional impulse and let us mistakenly believe that the value of free items is much higher than its actual value. This may be due to human instinctive fear of loss, and the true temptation of free is associated with this fear. There is no obvious loss in choosing a free item, but if the item we choose is not free, there is a risk that we may make a wrong decision and suffer a loss. So, if we let us choose, we will try to get it for free as much as we can.

Therefore, zero is not just a price, and the emotional impulse caused by free tokens is invincible. The price effect caused by zero is very special, it is unmatched by other figures.

Why are the unit costs of many project crowdfunding increasing over time? For example, in the first week of the project, there is a 40% discount, it is decreased by 10%

every week until the offer is no longer offered, and this is the use of free psychology to encourage investors to get in as soon as possible. And if you find this project in the fourth week and know the previous offers, then, even if you are interested in it, you are likely to choose to give up.

Let's give a simple example. A project (more reliable) is in the promotion period. After you register, you have two choices, and you can only choose one: one is to get the token worth 100 yuan for free, and the other is a token worth 200 yuan – you need to pay 70 yuan. Think about it right away, which one do you choose?

If you choose to get free 100 yuan token at once, then you are like the majority. If you count a little bit, you know that the token worth 200 yuan costs 70 yuan, so you earn 130 yuan. The income is definitely higher than the free 100 yuan token. Can you see the irrational behavior in reality?

From the project side point of view, through a wide range of airdrops, people who can get tokens can be motivated to understand and promote the project, so that the tokens in their hands will increase, which will become a common promotion method.

5.2.4 DAO Is Really the Main Form of Organization in the Future?

Recently, after careful research and analyses, you found a very good project, but according to some reasons, you don't have the right channel to participate, so you find a friend with broad opportunities to ask for help.

The friend readily agreed.

So you transferred him ten ETHs (this is the biggest asset you can use), and then, the friend transferred the token of the project to you a lot and even paid the transfer fee.

After 1 month, the project went on exchange and showed himself really good – there was a 50% increase in the cost price, so you made a profit.

So, you invited your friend for dinner to thank him.

You thanked him and took out the wallet: "This is 1000 RMB, please accept it".

How would the friends react? Would he be happy to accept the money, or would he smile very reluctantly? Even strike the table and leave?

Why is it that in some similar situations, to thank with money is not as simple as just to say "thank you" orally?

Social norms include good requests from each other. For example, when does this project start crowdfunding? How can I participate in this project? Social norms are hidden in our social nature and common needs. It is generally friendly and unclear, and does not require immediate returns. If you solve a problem for a person, it does not mean that he must help you to solve the problem right away, just like helping others to open the door – it brings joy to both of you and does not require immediate, equal return.

The other world is very different from this: it is ruled by market norms. There is no friendship here, and the boundaries are very clear. The exchange here is black and white: wages, prices, rent, interest, and costs and profits. This relationship is not necessarily evil and vulgar. In fact, it includes self-reliance, innovation, and individualism, but it does mean interest comparisons and immediate payments. If you are in a world dominated by market discipline, you have to pay for it by work – it has always been like this.

The fact that we live in both the social and market worlds is related to all aspects of our lives. From time to time, we need someone to help us move things, look after child for few hours, or receive a letter when we are out of town. How can we better motivate friends to help us? Or contribute to the community? It's hard to make decisions—especially when there's a danger of pushing relationships to market norms.

The subtle balance of social norms and market norms is also evident in the business world. For example, many companies try to establish social norms with their employees, because they see the advantage of creating atmosphere with social norms. With the continuous development of technology, the boundaries between work and leisure are becoming more and more blurred. The manager of the company wants us to think about work on the way home, even in the shower. So, we are equipped with laptops and mobile phones to eliminate the boundaries between the workplace and the family.

For companies, social norms have a greater advantage: they can make employees work enthusiastically and diligently, and care about the company. Employee loyalty to employers is often diminished under the market discipline, and social norms are the best way to motivate employees to remain loyal.

Open-source software shows the potential of social norms. In Linux (an operating system) and other collaborative projects, you can post questions on any forum, and soon there will be many people responding to your questions. People in these online communities are happy to contribute time to society as a whole.

Xiao Feng, the founder of Wanxiang Blockchain Labs, pointed out at the financial technology nighttime event on the sea:

> What issues are discussed by cryptoeconomics? First of all, we just talked about the operation of the entire blockchain. The economic organization on the block-chain neither depend on people, nor on companies, it depends on mathematical algorithms. Peer-to-peer trading also relies on mathematical algorithms. As you can see, a set of mathematical algorithms does not increase the marginal cost of one person and ten thousand people. Especially if the marginal cost tends to zero, then we still need the organizational system of "company"? The reason why the "company" was invented was necessary because the market transaction cost was too high, so it was necessary for us to internalize a certain part of the market function into an internal process to reduce the costs. The reason why companies can exist is because the cost of certain functions after internalization is lower than the market, so the existence of enterprises is necessary. When the marginal cost becomes zero, you don't need a company, because there is no point in its existence.

The community based on cryptoeconomics, or the decentralized organization, will better handle the relationship between social norms and market norms.

Perhaps in the future we will get used to a "society without money", which will completely abandon market norms: all activities in this community won't accept the coins. Instead of it, the entire community will commit the exchange economy – you give something to someone, and someone else will give you something. Here, everyone works hard for the same goal, developers will consciously contribute and update the necessary code, operators will publish articles and newsletters, designers will collect opinions from everyone to create products and pages, and everyone's labor will faithfully recorded on the blockchain, and according to it, you can get all the products and services the community can offer. This will be the most inclusive, socially caring community.

5.2.5 How to Control Our Impulses? Maybe You Need a Smart Contract

For many of us, rational consumption and rational investment is a hard thing: we know our monthly fixed income clearly, and we know that we should save in order to prevent accidents, but we still do not hesitate to make a purchase of the thing that we liked.

The same is for individual investors who focus on blockchain investment, if you look at any suggestions or guidelines for investing in blockchain projects, you will find that the primary emphasis is on reasonable asset allocation, which is generally at your disposal, usually 10%–20% of the budget surplus, but how many people really invest in this ratio?

I believe that there are a lot of people who quited their jobs and sold their houses to do investment in a full time fashion.

And that is not only about consumption and investment, our behavioral decisions in other areas are inconsistent with what we think.

When we are calm and rational, the estimation of behavioral decision is in line with a series of logical standards. How many people have said: "I speculate on the currency occasionally, so I won't put myself in". You think that you understand yourself, understand your preferences, and understand what you have the ability to do, but we often fail to estimate fully our response.

In Freud's terminology, each of us includes a dark "self", a "self", and a beast that gains control from the unpredictable "superego". As a result, friends who are usually calm and rational will be furious if they missed a good project and curse the project team; good-tempered people will become emotionally violent when the market plunges; people who only invest with their own pocket money will put all they can when Bitcoin skyrockets. These usually good people think that they know themselves, but when the market is extremely volatile, everything will be changed.

How can we deal with the irrationality that can emerge at any time?

Behavioral economists have shown through experiments that if there is an authoritarian "external voice" to issue orders, the majority of us will listen immediately;

but the best way seems to be to give people the opportunity to set their own bottom line and choose the path of action they like. This approach may not be as effective as mandatory, but it can help us to push ourselves in the right direction.

What is the bottom line? We have difficulties in self-control, which is related to immediate satisfaction and delayed satisfaction – this is a clear fact. But at the same time, every problem we face has a potential self-control mechanism. If we can't withdraw from the wages we receive, we may let the employer automatically help us deduct it; if we don't control how much money we invest in the currency market, we can be supervised by others. There are many tools that allow us to achieve self-control and help us achieve our aspirations.

Yes, I believe that the concept of "smart contract" has already emerged in your mind. It can help us to control our behavior by setting up smart contracts.

For example, spending with credit card. Many years ago, the United States had an "ice cup" method that can reduce credit card spending. This can be the way to correct the impulse of consumption in your own home: you put your credit card in a glass of water and then put it in the refrigerator to freeze it. Then, if you are impulsive and decide to buy something, you must wait for the ice in the cup melted to take the credit card. By that time, your impulses may disappear.

Of course, for those of you who have countless credit cards and have already opened Jiebei and Huabei, it is not a good idea to put credit card and mobile phone into a refrigerator. It is simply a smart contract that provides us with a new solution, and it has created a more effective mechanism for us, both free choice and inherent limitations.

Imagine a credit card with a smart agreement written in advance that can help you to limit your consumer behavior. You can set the spending limit for each type of item, each store, and each purchase. For example, you can limit snack consumption to 300 USD per month, cloth consumption to 2,000 USD per quarter, and entertainment consumption to 200 USD per month, and prohibit spending on desserts at 10 o'clock in the evening.

What if you exceed the spending limit? It's up to you to decide what kind of punishment you can take, such as setting up a credit card to automatically repay, or transfer to regular savings, donate to a charity, or even automatically post it to your Facebook moments like the following:

"Yes, I once again broke my promises. I did not insist on my own budget control plan at 23:12 on February 22, 2020 because I ordered a barbecue takeaway and a bottle of Coke. Please watch and help me".

Imagine the potential of credit cards with smart contracts that are beginning to flood into the market. These smart cards offer the possibility to create consumption plans according to each person's needs and help people manage credit wisely. Of course, there could be created other tools with smart contracts similar to it, and it will help us to control our lives better.

5.2.6 *Dilemma of Multiple Choices: Why Do We Want to Participate in All Projects?*

2017 is a year of digital currency and ICO outbreak. Anyone who from cryptocommunity can easily name a few sky-rocketing currencies. Income in hundreds of thousands has completely ignited our passion for ICO.

Have you ever had such an experience: as you didn't have the opportunity to participate in public crowdfunding of skyrocketing project, you don't want to miss any possible project anymore, so you don't care about your original work every day, but you all the time check everything about the latest projects, joined hundreds of project investment discussion groups, and you are not afraid of hard work of leafing through the phone?

However, our energy is limited, our funds are limited, it is impossible to participate in all projects, and not all projects are reliable.

However, even if you completely agree with this, but you see someone in the group is sending information about new project, or if you create a new project QR code, you will still naturally join the group and then open the group settings, and cancel group message reminder, of course, if this project is really promising, you will top it.

In fact, not only projects but also many people are concerned about the situation with prices of hundreds of currencies – although they hold less than one-tenth. So, what is the reason for us to pay attention to the information about all projects?

In the context of today's world, we still try our best to keep a variety of choices for ourselves, and sometimes we even may not know that we missed other things during this process. While you are terribly busy with something not necessarily important, you can forget about something that really matters. The result is that as you were focused on too many projects, you couldn't do in-depth study of several very good projects and missed investment opportunities.

What are the consequences of the situation when there are a lot of choices? Why do we have to keep so many choices for ourselves, even if these choices have to pay a very high price? Why can't we do everything intently?

Shen Jiying, professor at Yale University, experiments found out that usually in case of clear target guidance, we will strive to pursue the maximum satisfaction. In the ideal situation, we will try all possible options and then choose the most suitable one. However, the facts are not so ideal, because the opportunity is fleeting, you can't wait until all the projects are analyzed and then require the project to start crowdfunding, so you will always miss some of them; of course, the best projects may be among them.

How can we get rid of this irrational impulse and not chase the redundant choices that are worthless? The philosopher Erich Fromm wrote a book in 1941, *Escape from Freedom*. He said that under the modern democratic system, it is not the lack of opportunities, but there are too many opportunities, and it makes people dazzling. Now it is more evident in today's society. People constantly remind themselves that we can do everything and achieve what we expect.

The question is whether this dream can be achieved. We must do everything possible to improve ourselves; we must try everything in life; we must look at all the 1,000 things at least once before we are born. And if we do like this, will you not be overworked and exhausted?

It is necessary for us to give up these projects simply because these projects are time-consuming and crowd out our participation opportunities, and they make us unable to take into account those valuable choices and make us exhausted.

5.3 The Intersection of Behavioral Economics and Cryptoeconomics

Above, we can recognize that in daily life and behavioral decision-making, we are not as rational and comprehensive as traditional economics, and smart contracts in cryptographic economics can be used as external constraints to help us do better. The decision-making, the fair and open nature of the blockchain itself allows us to get the information we want to know, rather than the data being controlled by a third-party intermediary.

We can predict that with the constant development of blockchain technology and the gradual improvement of the theory of cryptoeconomics, we will come to a better world, what that is to be considered by the companies that want to enter this field.

Chapter 6

Cryptoeconomics and the Security of Blockchain

Cryptoeconomics is easily associated with economics in the real world. They have similarities, but they are not exactly the same. Our real economics is more about studying the laws of economic operation in society, such as studying how people make choices, which makes it easier for policies to better coordinate economic and social progress and development. And cryptoeconomics is more about a mechanism design (mechanism design, a branching field that combines microeconomics and game theory). We can understand this simply: cryptoeconomics is to re-enact a framework and rules that are economically efficient in the world of encryption, and everything here is based on code and contains a reasonable incentive system. Therefore, cryptoeconomics is more about the design. And economics in reality is more about discovering laws from the existing social structure and following them.

From another point of view, the economic laws in the real world will be affected by many factors. In the encrypted digital world, all the operating rules have been determined by the code, and most of the code rules are mainly open source, that is to say the last chain that can be left is the one that gains the majority of consensus. This also reflects its fairness, while also taking into account the most important – trustworthiness.

Of course, it is not enough to justify fairness and credibility, because everything here is built on another, most important premise: security.

Since it is seen as the Internet of value in the future, how to ensure that the value has a 100% steel-like protection in decentralized systems, this is a top priority. Below, let us first understand the main factors affecting security in the cryptoeconomics system.

6.1 Sybil Attack

The name "Sybil attack" originates from the film based on Flora Rhea Schreiber's novel *Sybil*, written in 1973. This was a story about the psychotherapy of the woman with pseudonym Sybil Dorsett. She was diagnosed with a dissociative identity disorder, and she used to have 16 personalities.

The extended meaning of this word is that in a peer-to-peer network, a node usually has multiple identities, which weaken the role of redundant backups by controlling most of the nodes of the system.

In a peer-to-peer network, that is, a P2P network, because different users can join or exit node at any time, in order to maintain network stability, the same data will be backed up to multiple distributed nodes. This is what we call "data redundancy mechanism". The ultimate goal of sybil attack is to attack the data redundancy mechanism.

The main accounting confirmation of the Bitcoin network is maintained by the power provided by the miners. Let's assume that a miner in the network needs to change the rules and results of the network for some purpose, such as the speed of making the block (we can't guarantee that every miner is trustworthy), and if such a miner is planning to achieve the goal, then he can invest a lot of computing power or buy other miners to achieve the goal.

So-called investing a huge amount of computing power has a very simple logics, it is just to buy mining machine hardware and produce computing power, but in this case, the cost will be huge. If you want to control the Bitcoin network, according to recent currency price of Bitcoin, you will need at least 3–4 billion dollars. This way of controlling the right to update the entire network is also called 51% right.

Let's take a look at the second case. If enough miners unite to modify the results, it is considered as malicious behavior. If the evil miners have enough people to unite, they can concentrate only on the transactions they want to process transactions and ignore other transactions.

The network with low-level redundancy has the risk of being attacked by sybils at any time. Several large miners can collude at any time, destroying the network with greater than or almost 51% of computing power (the right of making the blocks), and not packing or not putting the blocks on the ledger in the critical moment is already fatal. Once a malicious node obtained the right to put the blocks on the ledger freely, we can say that the sybil attack is successful. At the same time, it can also be declared that the entire network will become untrustworthy and lose its value.

Although the principle of sybil attack is simple, we cannot completely eliminate this phenomenon. Once the right to put the block on the ledger is monopolized by a few people, they may betray at any time and shift from trustworthy node to a sybil attacker.

6.1.1 Cost of Sybil Attacks on Traditional and Blockchain Networks

The previous section briefly illustrates the principles of sybil attacks on blockchain networks. In fact, in terms of sybil attacks, it is easier to attack on a traditional network. It is easier because of the cost. Since the cost of launching a sybil attack in a traditional network is extremely low, a malicious attacker will have a relatively large profit if the attack is successfully executed. Take a step back and say that there is no loss even if there is no success.

From an economic point of view, everything has costs, and the value is not worth doing. Cost is an important factor. On the other hand, we are familiar only with the bitcoin network; since 2009, we have been running safely without any centralized management. This is because the cost of the problem has been taken into account when Nakamoto was designing it. In other words, if you are going to carry out a sybil attack on the Bitcoin network, then you have to pay for it. And the cost is not low.

At least you have to have computing power (i.e., a mining machine), and you have to pay a high cost of electricity. So, a malicious node with a profit-making purpose will find that it is not cost-effective; perhaps you will think about whether there will be such a malicious node, which is not doing that for profit, but for just disrupting the network or for crashing? In fact, you only need to know a little more so you can understand that you have to pay at least $3 billion on hardware costs to control the bitcoin network. Here is only the cost of purchasing equipment directly. If you want to bribe different miners for malicious attacks, then you must pay more than normal mining to achieve the goal.

Here, the role of economic law is so powerful that it basically eliminates the way of hoping to shut down the bitcoin network through sybil attacks. This is also the ingenuity of cryptoeconomics.

Of course, because the bitcoin network is too powerful now, the sybil attack definitely has a very small probability of success. However, the newly emerged network may not be so lucky. Due to insufficient network computing power and insufficient nodes, the probability of sybil attack success would be much greater. There are few projects that were dead because of sybil attack.

The prevention of sybil attacks is the game of putting the transaction in a new block. The more people participate in the event, the less likely they are to collude; for example, they are from different countries and different interest groups. Therefore, the more the participants, the safer the network. However, it raises a problem. When the network wants to upgrade, the original competitive contradiction will improve the resistance of the software. Just like a double-edged sword, how to use and balance interests is a problem that needs to be continuously explored from the perspective of cryptoeconomics in the future blockchain network consensus mechanism.

6.2 Fork: Soft Fork and Hard Fork

6.2.1 Fork, Soft Fork, and Hard Fork Concepts

Fork is a by-product of distributed consensus; it happens when two miners produce blocks at almost the same time. This uncertainty disappears when subsequent blocks are added to one of the blocks. It makes this chain the longest, and the other block is "isolated" or "abandoned" by the network. In addition, with the development of bitcoin, the bugs of various bitcoins need to be repaired, and the bitcoin protocol needs to be continuously improved. The bitcoin network is continuously upgraded by the forks. However, the Bitcoin network is not the same as the original centralized software. The original centralized software only needs to upgrade the software of the central node, and the upgrade of the Bitcoin network can only be carried out by the fork. Forks are divided into soft fork and hard forks. Soft fork and hard fork are two ways to upgrade the Bitcoin network. When developers want to modify Bitcoin's consensus algorithm, they can also voluntarily fork the network. When a block contains an invalid transaction, the block will be ignored by the network and the miners who find the block will lose the blockchain reward. So usually the miners just want to dig into the effective block and join the longest chain.

1. Fork

   In the blockchain, the miner creates the block and links it to the main chain. Generally, only one block is generated at the same time. If two blocks are generated at the same time, there will emerge two blockchains of the same length and with the same information about transactions in the whole network, but with different miners' signatures or different transaction order. This situation is called fork. The blockchain branches into two different chains with the same "ancestors".

2. Soft Fork

   Soft forks are forward-compatible forks in blockchain or decentralized systems. Forward compatibility means that when a new consensus rule is released, the node does not have to be upgraded to a new consensus rule in the decentralized structure, because the new rules for soft forks still conform to the old rules, and all nodes that are not upgraded still can accept new rules. In this case, there are no complete nodes executing the old rules, and there are no miners who produce the blocks that conform to traditional rules. All complete nodes have been upgraded to enforce soft fork rules, and all miners are producing blocks that meet the soft fork rules. Therefore, the chain does not fork. This is the soft fork blockchain.

3. Hard Fork

Hard fork refers to a fork that is not forward compatible in a blockchain or decentralized network. Hard forks always change the technology used by cryptocurrency. This change makes all new data blocks different from the original ones. The old version will not accept the blocks created by the new version. If a new hard fork fails, then all users will get back to original data. An example of a hard fork is the breakup of Bitcoin's New York Consensus in 2017, which eventually split bitcoin into BCH and increased the block size limit from 1 MB to 8 MB. Although the 8 MB block was previously considered to be an incompatible block in the bitcoin network, it was compatible with 8 MB blocks after hard fork activation.

Another well-known fork case is the hard fork of The DAO on Ethereum, which is the best analytical example to show the disagreement in community rules. The original etheric chain turned into two different versions of the blockchain – ETC and ETH, each with a different concept and token.

6.2.2 *Main Characteristics of Soft Fork and Hard Fork*

1. Characteristics of soft fork

   Soft fork has following characteristics:
   1. It doesn't create a new chain.
   2. Due to the limitation of transaction data and block data structure, complex rule changes such as changing the block size cannot be implemented through soft forks.
   3. Convenient to implement (it doesn't require upgrade from you).

2. Characteristics of hard fork

   Hard fork has the following characteristics:
   1. It creates a new chain.
   2. Do not consider the compatibility of the old node with the new node, and make serious changes in the transaction data and the block data structure.
   3. The implementation is relatively complicated (the miners who do not upgrade the nodes remain on the original branch).

6.2.3 *The Importance of Forks*

From the current mainstream point of view, the overall opinion about the fork is positive. Since the soft forks create limited changes to the network, the main focus is on the changes that the hard forks bring to the entire ecosystem.

1. Forked chains can add new technical features.

   The most famous bitcoin fork should belong to the "forked out" bitcoin cash BCH. The important reason here is resentment between the Bitmain and Core teams. Bitmain is currently the world's largest mining pool. Due to the lack of consensus on block expansion and isolation certification, Bitcoin decided that Bitcoin Cash (BCH) was completed after the network block reached a height of 504,031 and it completed a hard fork. After that, BCH updated the network difficulty adjustment algorithm DAA and increased the block capacity from 1M to 8M. After the BCH forked, there were plenty of forked coins, each of them with its own updated features. Therefore, we can see that the hard fork is actually a process of bringing innovation to the whole ecosystem. Since Satoshi's invention of Bitcoin, there has been no restriction on the hard fork behavior of Bitcoin. The various forked out bitcoins with different characteristics are fully compatible on the market and are chosen the most suitable currency for people.

2. Relations between forks and community

   Fork is the result of a consensus that cannot be achieved. In the above example, the Bitcoin community could not reach an agreement, which led to the bitcoin blockchain fork. What if I can't complete the fork? Unfortunately, if there is no way to solve it through the fork, it may lead to the team take different roads. For example, we are familiar with the case the BitShares founder BM (Dan Larimer), when it was impossible to reach a consensus with the community, and finally, he could only leave the team.

Therefore, whether from innovation or community stability point of view, hard forks have rationality and positive sides in their own existence.

Due to the poor performance of Ethereum in dealing with high concurrency cases, Vitalik is already considering the PoS consensus mechanism, but if this may touch the interests of a large number of original miners, will it be resolved by hard forks at the end?

6.3 P + ε Attack

In the real world, it is always difficult to judge whether a person is a good person or a bad person, and whether a person is selfish or altruistic. In the democratic world, the minority obeying the majority is already a common consensus. But is it reasonable to be the result of the majority's approval? We first rule out the irrational behavior of individuals who are emotionally affected. We assume that everyone chooses for their own interests and then realize that even a seemingly fair democratic voting system contains many unfair or even wrong.

For example, Arrow's impossibility theorem in economics mainly includes two points.

1. Even in case of a fair vote, the vote does not necessarily reflect the wishes of the majority.

2. Simultaneous voting is easily guided by the host to the desired result.

To avoid such problems, it is necessary to cast money instead of votes. If there is a problem in a fair voting environment and the vote is manipulated, then it is clear that in the end, general public will suffer from it.

Therefore, this is also the greatest significance of the decentralized blockchain network, so that all accounts and elections are open and transparent. This is also the goal which is pursued by people.

Similarly, the laws of the economy in the real world are similar to those in cryptoeconomics. In the blockchain world, each node has to make constant choices to confirm which block is real; this is also a voting process. This process may be exploited by malicious nodes, for example, with a bribery. The $P + \varepsilon$ attack mentioned here is just one of such processes.

6.3.1 What Is $P + \varepsilon$ Attack

Suppose there is a simple Schelling game in which the user votes to determine the outcome of a particular fact, the truth is (1) false (0).

At this point, each user can vote according to their own knowledge: 1 or 0. If the user's option is consistent with the majority in voting, the user will receive the reward P; otherwise, there will be no reward. We can show it in a payoff matrix diagram, as shown in Figure 6.1.

	Individual votes 0	Individual votes 1
The majority votes 0	P	0
The majotiry votes 1	0	P

Figure 6.1　Payoff Matrix without ε.

The theoretical logic here is that if everyone wants others to vote truly, then their motivation is to vote honestly in respect for the majority, and that is why people believe and are willing to vote for those chose by majority; in this case, the system reaches a self-enhancing Nash equilibrium.

Here, we can see if the individual votes for 0 and the result comes out, the majority vote is also 0 and then the individual can get the reward P; if the individual votes for 1, the majority vote will be 0, and the individual will not be rewarded.

The other two cases are similar.

Obviously, this is an ideal state. So, if there are dishonest or even evil voters in the system?

Now, let's see if there is an attack. Suppose an attacker with sufficient financial strength promises (if there is enough money, it will let others trust him). If the result of the vote is 0, then the voter of the vote will be paid $P + \varepsilon$ (the voter who gives the minority vote). If the result of the vote is 1 win, no fee will be paid (not voting for the majority vote). Figure 6.2 shows the payoff matrix.

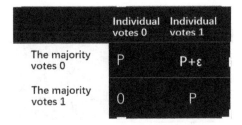

	Individual votes 0	Individual votes 1
The majority votes 0	P	P+ε
The majority votes 1	0	P

Figure 6.2   Payoff Matric with ε.

For the voter: if the voter is rational, this multiple-choice question is very simple, because choosing to vote for 1 is the most in line with his own interests, because the worst result of the vote is to get the reward P. If you are lucky, you may get P + ε (Figure 6.2).

For the attacker: once this cheating is successful, the attacker can achieve the goal without paying any fees. It is quite simple, if option 1 that was not recognized by the public is persuaded by many attackers to vote, and it becomes the final result, then according to the agreement, only if the result shows option 1 as a minority, P + ε can be obtained.

It must be said that logically speaking, the P + ε attack is a very good way to attack. Just from the current point of view, this way still costs a lot, so the question is whether you really need to do this.

6.3.2 Protection from P + ε Attacks

In fact, Vitalik, the founder of Ethereum, has already analyzed this problem since 2015 that was one of the important reasons for the planned upgrade of Ethereum to Casper.

Casper has a lot of contents, and those who are interested can search online. For now, we just need to know that it is based on a PoS consensus mechanism.

We can see from the above example that the biggest problem with $P + \varepsilon$ is that an attacker can organize an attack without paying in advance. He just needs to prove that he has enough ability to pay. In Casper, the voting weight of any voter will be directly related to the assets that it holds. In other words, you have to be forced to mortgage some of your assets (the Ethereum is the mortgage of Ethereum coins) to the system before making a choice, and the amount of this asset decides you rights for voice. This will greatly increase the cost of malicious behavior. Each voter can only choose the true result to make a choice. If you want to change the result and invest in the minority, then you may not only get the reward but also lose all the mortgage and your assets.

In this case, if the perpetrator wants to buy other voters, he can only show more of his assets in order to gain the trust of the others.

6.4 DAO Attack

Regarding Dao attacks, we have to first understand the history of this story.

On July 30, 2015, Vitalik Buterin and the Ethereum Foundation created the first blockchain-based Turing Complete Smart Contract Platform. On this day, Ethereum officially met the public. Then, Sock.it designed The DAO Ethereum Contract and officially deployed The Dao Smart Contract on April 30, 2016. On May 27, 2016, it has completed the world's largest crowdfunding raising $150 million.

On June 17, 2016, The DAO was hacked and stolen a large amount of Ethereum (3,641,694 ETH). This is the famous Dao attack. It is precise because of this attack that the original Ethereum was harmed a lot, and finally, in desperation, in order to save the loss of The DAO's investors, it was decided to make a hard fork. On July 20, 2016, at the block height of 1,920,000 it was successfully hard-forked. The abandoned original chain is the current classical ETC.

Looking back at history, this Dao attack is supposed to be very powerful, and its destructive power almost destroyed Ethereum. On the day when it was announced that money were stolen, Ethereum price slumped by 50%.

So what is the DAO attack?

The attacker exploited a fatal vulnerability in the contract. The attacker created a contract to allocate the split-DAO of The DAO Contract and exploited the vulnerability to let The DAO Smart Contract call the "()" function in the attacker's new contract, and then recursively allocated splitDAO in the function. That didn't stop until the gas was fully used up, or the memory stacklimit was reached, or the recursion limit was reached. Before this, it was possible to transfer account balance without reducing your own.

Now that this vulnerability has been fixed, I believe that there will be no such recursive calls.

6.4.1 The Significance of The DAO Cryptoeconomics

In a sense, The DAO is the most important significant social experiment since Bitcoin. In a world where everyone is got used to centralized management, how to achieve decentralized management?

First let's look at the development from the very beginning to the launch of the project:

1. A group of people wrote smart contracts (programs) for the organization they want to run
2. There was an initial funding period during which people were providing funding sources to DAO by purchasing tokens that represent ownership (known as crowdfunding or ICO).
3. After the end of fundraising, DAO began to operate.
4. People could make recommendations to DAO on how to use the funds, and members holding tokens can vote for them.

It can be seen that from programming, to fundraising and then to decision-making, it is based on the principle of being as decentralized as possible. In fact, it is also an important universality of our discussion about cryptoeconomics: decentralization. Due to this feature, people should consider not just the code problem when designing an organization like DAO, since the code supports the distributed feature. The Dao's vision is to achieve autonomy in the community through distribution, decentralization, and this vision is very good, but if there is no security guarantee, even more ambitious dream also can vanish.

This is a fair side, but The DAO attack also shows us that there were problems based on this economic design:

1. After the accident has happened, the decentralized system met a dilemma in response. For example, if the solution is submitted late, it will be complained by public opinion; but the quick solution will lead to more centralization, and because it is impossible to take into account everyone, it will be partially resisted.

2. The perpetrators are hard to be traced and even pursued. First, because there is no special legal constraint, the second is that the method used by the perpetrators in theory is not prohibited by the system. It may take more time to perfect the contract from a software algorithm pint of view.

3. The software is open source, so the people who provide the code are scattered around the world. Is there a malicious programmer? Can you accept anonymous contributions? In a decentralized community, who is responsible for the software?

4. Mine work is an important part of the blockchain ecosystem. It is very easy to generate centralized gathering. But how to assign reasonable rewards to miners and limit their influence? In the solution of The DAO, if there is no support from the miners, it may lead another completely different result.

The reason why we need to decentralize is because we believe that there is no perfect person, and then we have to seriously think over a question: is there a perfect code?

There are still many problems. The DAO attack is essentially a technical error, but from the perspective of cryptoeconomics, it may be more like a system problem or even a philosophical problem.

6.5 Zero-Knowledge Proof

The "zero-knowledge proof" was proposed by S. Goldwasser, S. Micali, and C. Rackoff in the early 1980s. It means that the certifier is able to believe that a certain assertion is correct without providing any useful information to the verifier. A zero-knowledge proof is essentially an agreement involving two or more parties, where two or more parties take series of steps that are required for finishing the task. The certifier proves to the verifier and believes that he or she knows or owns a message, but the attestation process cannot disclose any information about the certified message to the verifier. A large number of facts prove that zero-knowledge proof is very useful in cryptography. If you can use zero-knowledge proof for verification, you will be able to solve many problems effectively.

There are a lot of projects with zero-knowledge proof design, but probably the most famous is Zcash.

Here's a simple example. If you pick up a wallet and someone is claiming it, you can prove that this person is the real wallet owner in two ways:

1. Let the other party provide evidence of the owner of the wallet, or if it happens to have an ID card in the wallet, it can be proved immediately.
2. There is no document in the wallet. You can let the other party describe the details of the wallet. If you can describe it in detail, such as how much money there is, the color of the wallet, approximate time when it was lost and where it was lost, etc...., you can also prove it.

The second option is zero-knowledge proof. In other words, the purpose of zero-knowledge proof is to let you ask the sender to protect his privacy and to implement the transaction without publishing his identity.

Under the mechanism of zero-knowledge proof, only the transaction amount is disclosed to the counterparty in the personal information, and all other information is known only for you. But why is it good? Here, we have to talk about the trading mechanism of Bitcoin. We know that in the Bitcoin network, your public key is open to everyone, which means that once your address is exposed, in theory everyone can know how much money do you have there. Moreover, it will be not only the deposit at this address, but also the deposits of all addresses that have been trading with this address. After all these descriptions, are you be able to feel the seriousness of the problem here?

The WannaCry virus incident in 2017 has caused many victims to pay bitcoin to redeem their files. We can imagine that if hackers specifically attack and exploit addresses in the future, it will cause even greater losses. Therefore, if you want to store a lot of bitcoins, unless you never connect to the Internet with this address; you will always be tailed. Privacy of your bitcoins has become an important issue. Zero-knowledge proof can solve this problem well, and unless you disclose it, the payee cannot know your sending address and identity.

From the perspective of cryptoeconomics, there are two contradictions that are difficult to reconcile. First, the ledger disclosure of the blockchain can better form a consensus. Second, if an address is stolen, a certain clue can always be found through the common search of the parties. However, once the sending and receiving addresses are hidden, in case of asset theft, there is basically no way to trace them. How people choose is still unknown nowadays, and freedom and responsibility is a problem that everyone needs to think about.

Summary

Human beings are constantly pursuing freedom and equality. For the first time, the emergence of Bitcoin gives almost everyone the freedom to control their wealth and create wealth equally. But this premise is to have security as a guarantee, and no one will give up security for freedom.

We discussed several major security issues that happened in the current blockchain asset world. These are not all of them, and there may be more threats in the future.

The threat we encounter may come from technology and possibly from system. We have to jump out of the limitations of a single technical thinking, and it is a reasonable approach to consider the various components of the entire cryptoeconomics circle systematically, and how to balance the power, responsibility, and profit in all aspects of this cryptoeconomics Eco circle is a long and serious test for it.

The participation of this system is following:

■ Code creation (open source): how to use positive incentives in order to motivate software writers not to conduct malicious behavior?

■ Maintenance of the project: How to make the maintainer escape centralization while guaranteeing its own interests?

■ System security maintenance (miners): How can we make reasonable rewards and a larger distributed structure?

■ Consumer: How to make it easy for users to use and keep assets safe?

■ Investors and Communities: How to reduce speculation and create a positive community culture?

Therefore, this ideal system allows the parties to restrict and develop each other through reasonable design, and at the same time, the perpetrators outside the system cannot gain benefits from their own acts of evil.

From now on, the Bitcoin network is a reasonable balance of resources. The important point is that the network is simple enough, so external attacks are hard to come by. Although the public questioned the high concentration of miners, it has not yet reached the level of centralization. We can also think further, if we achieve centralization and then conduct malicious behavior after investing a lot of financial resources, then the loss of the perpetrators will certainly be enormous. Why? Because, in addition to financial input, another certain intangible loss is that once the malicious behavior is successful, the bitcoin network will no longer be credible, which may lead to the current high-value instant zero return. From this point of view, no individual or organization with the ultimate goal of interest has any motivation to do this.

Although we are still experiencing this or that safety dangers, we believe that as long as human beings keep exploring, there will be methods of solution in the future.

Chapter 7

Blockchain in China

7.1 The Power of Blockchain in Real Life

Today, blockchain technology is considered to be the most disruptive technological innovation since the invention of the Internet. Without the intervention of any third-party center, participants can reach a consensus and solve the problem of reliable transmission of trust and value at a very low cost.

The security characteristics and trust mechanism of the blockchain is becoming an important technological engine for the development of the digital economy. It can play a role in various industries. The development potential of the industry application field is huge, and it is expected to reshape all spheres of life. According to Gartner's forecast, the market value of blockchain technology will reach $176 billion in 2025 and reach $3.1 trillion by 2030.

Nowadays, there are plenty of successful cases of blockchain used in different industries, and they already brought obvious economic and social benefits.

For example, in the financial sector blockchain has been used in supply chain finance, blockchain credit, blockchain insurance, judicial electronic information deposit, and billing. It is applied in many other industries, such as culture products and copyright management, trading, agricultural product traceability, security information exchange in the network, police data exchange, blockchain medical association, blockchain real estate deposit certificate, blockchain electronic invoices, blockchain enterprise tax database, blockchain poverty alleviation, and fund management.

7.2 Real Use Cases of Blockchain in China

7.2.1 Financial Solutions

The financial industry is inherently rich in many raw data and needs a large-scale consensus, so it complies with the needs in the financial sector.

For example, **supply chain finance**. Traditional supply chain finance has many problems, such as information is fragmented, enterprise credit cannot be transmitted, and compliance risk is difficult to control effectively. The blockchain completes credit transmission based on shared books and uses timestamp technology, so it is difficult to tamper with features to realize transaction confirmation and transaction real proof. It provides automated operational tools for supply chain financial business execution based on smart contracts.

In March 2017, JD Finance launched an infrastructure asset management platform for asset cloud factory based on blockchain technology; it aimed to help companies in financial services for JD consumer supply chain to land in JD Finance's asset cloud plant business. The system has set up three verification nodes: application, approval, loan; other capital flow of each loan in the bottom asset pool has to pass through every verification node on the blockchain; and the cash flow information is directly linked into the chain through its designated payment channel, ensuring the strong coupling between the generation and circulation of the underlying assets and the blockchain, and guaranteeing the consistency between the incoming assets and the assets out of the chain. At the same time, the information and funds of various institutions are kept in real time through distributed ledgers and consensus mechanisms, effectively solving the problem of time-consuming and laborious reconciliation and clearing between institutions.

In 2018, Tencent also took its focus on Supply Chain Finance Solution. On April 12, 2018, the Tencent blockchain officially released the "Tencent Blockchain + Supply Chain Financial Solution". It has fundamentally improved the financing dilemma of small and microenterprises and contributed to the transformation of the local industry and upgrading through application of the blockchain technology and operational resources of Tencent. It has used the accounts receivable of the core enterprise as the underlying assets, and realized the circulation of credit certificates through Tencent's blockchain technology, to ensure that the relevant information cannot be falsified, cannot be refinanced, can be traced, and can help related parties form a supply chain.

In the credit information industry, there has been a row of disadvantages as a relatively narrow circle of market participants, limited coverage of public credit reporting agencies, and personal information security issues. And application of blockchain in this industry is used to complete **the credit information on chain**, so it guarantees that the original data is non-tamperable. Just like that, Gongxinbao in 2016 has developed a "Gongxinbao Data Exchange", a universal data exchange, based on blockchain technology. The bottom layer is an alliance chain based on the blockchain (public chain). The typical customers are Internet finance companies, government departments, banks, and insurance companies. *Gongxinbao* mainly collects user data under the authorization of users through data crawler products, covering various dimensions such as pan-finance, pan-e-commerce, pan-social, and personal identity, providing credit basis for major banks, Internet finance companies, and other institutions. *Gongxinbao* will anonymize the parties of the transaction, realize the ownership certification of digital assets, and effectively curb the fraud in data exchange.

In 2016, *Bubi*, one of the leaders in applying blockchain technologies to different industries within the Chinese market, reached a strategic agreement with

Tiancheng Credit, aiming to build a general-purpose credit information system through blockchain decentralized mutual assistance and cooperation, and a network-wide accounting system, and use the consensus mechanism of blockchain to establish open credit. The blockchain credit solution designed by both parties is that the data part stored in the blockchain is publicly visible, and users in need can find the required data through search and purchase it from all data vendors. The program will solve the problem of trust and transaction difficulties between data providers, and reduce the procedures and costs of data transactions.

According to incomplete statistics, more than 20% of the ongoing blockchain application scenarios in the world involve insurance. Although the application of blockchain technology in the insurance industry is mostly in the technical verification stage, the rapid development of the application scenario has already predicted that the technology will bring a transformative impact to the **insurance industry**. According to the survey, more than half of the insurance companies' executives around the world have recognized the importance of blockchain technology for the insurance industry.

The essence of insurance is risk trading, which can serve the real economy naturally, but the insurance industry faces major challenges such as data dispersion and data security. The blockchain can realize information sharing and connection of a large number of distributed nodes based on shared accounts. Blockchain ensures that the insurance service process is more transparent, and it uses smart contracts to automate business processes. In that way, China Construction Bank and technology giant IBM have jointly developed a bank insurance service system based on blockchain technology.

Another interesting example is the *Shanghai Stock Exchange Blockchain Insurance Service Platform*, which was launched in September 2017. This platform independently developed the Golang national secret algorithm package, which can support 50,000 fingerprint data verification chaining per second in the electronic policy deposit certificate scenario and can respond to high concurrent system requests. This system can be widely used in insurance transactions, financial clearing and settlement, and anti-fraud and regulatory compliance.

According to the public information, the main service structure of the insurance chain includes four aspects: the consensus service architecture ensures the consistency of the data on the chain; the identity authentication service architecture implements such functions of authentication as authentication, auditing, issue, and management of identity data. Under the premise of ensuring the security of smart contracts, the contract service architecture implements the service functions of installing, applying and upgrading smart contracts, which provides strong support for the authentication services in the blockchain system; the platform service architecture satisfies the dynamics. Multi-chain configuration and access mode services under the same network and the same underlying platform. At the same time, the chain supports three functions of data security and cleaning, application scenario system, and data exchange service.

7.2.2 Police and Other Governmental Solutions

China officially stresses upon the key values of justice and fairness. The transparent traceable network constructed by blockchain technology complies with these values of justice and fairness, and at the same time can improve judicial efficiency and embody judicial procedural justice. In the legal field, the blockchain can be applied to invoicing, collecting evidence, electronic data, PoE, and public security data.

In 2012, The Law of Civil Procedure approved collecting evidence (取证) for the first time, and collecting evidence started to be used as a valid evidence. However, the main problem in this field is electronic data authenticity and integrity. As the main feature of blockchain is traceability, it can solve these problems and ensure the authenticity of electronic data. Zhejiang DataQin company developed the security network chain for that purpose. In the case of a dispute over the infringement of the information network communication right in the Hangzhou Internet Court, one of the parties used this security network to collect evidence. After the trial, the court approved the blockchain application in keeping electronic data. During this case, blockchain was recognized for the first time in the Chinese Court.

The other problem which exists in judicial fields is **data sharing** between different judicial organizations. For example, according to the existing law system, three organizations of public security are independent from each other and that influence efficiency and accuracy of the work. Blockchain can contribute a lot in this field, can realize data sharing on the chain based on the shared ledger, and connect the public security, the procuratorate, and the court that can improve the efficiency of case integration. Guizhou Ruipu Political and Legal Big Data Platform has been used since 2016, and only 2.3% of cases were given back for supplementary investigation (when there are not enough evidence), and it has decreased 25.7% in comparison with the previous year; the arrest rate due to insufficient evidence has dropped 28.8% year-on-year in comparison with the previous year, the level acquittal decisions because of lack of evidence became close to zero, and the time limit for handling cases was shortened by nearly 30%. The chain landed in Guiyang, Sichuan, and Guangzhou.

Another interesting example is *Arbitrage Chain*. In February 2018, the first "blockchain + PoE" award based on blockchain technology was issued by the Guangzhou Arbitration Commission. The so-called *Arbitrage Chain* has been operating stably for 5 months and has been built by WeBank in collaboration with the Guangzhou Arbitration Commission and Hangzhou Yibei Technology company. *Arbitrage Chain* is based on blockchain and helps to prevent tampering, and it is trustworthy, distributive, and based on encryption algorithms. When the data is signed and confirmed by the consensus mechanism, the chain is supplemented by smart contracts to ensure the authenticity of the data, so it can guarantee legality, relevance requirements, and standardization of trials and evidence.

When it comes to the matter, the user's authentication result and the HASH of the business operation evidence will be recorded on the *Arbitrage Chain* (legal chain block). When arbitration is required, the background personnel only need to click a button, and the corresponding evidence will be transmitted to the arbitration platform. After the arbitration institution receives the data, it checks with the blockchain node to verify the data and verifies it according to the network arbitration rules and issues an arbitral award.

A consensus and real-time evidence, in case of disputes, are verified with PoE data and can be regarded as a direct evidence, reducing the arbitration process and costs, and improving.

7.2.3 *Food Safety and Supply Chain*

The problem of food safety has been a very hot topic in media for a very long time. Food safety incidents such as waste oil, toxic milk powder, so-called "zombie meat", and cadmium rice are numerous. The blockchain is based on decentralization and traceability, and can be transparent, so it can create a traceable system and an "unbreakable" food safety chain. In this way, on December 14, 2017, Wal-Mart,

JD, IBM, and Tsinghua University jointly established *Safe Food Blockchain Traceability Alliance*, which aims to improve food tracking and safety by using blockchain. This cooperation between the four parties has created an effective standard for China to be a food safety ecosystem. Among them, IBM uses its own platform to provide expertise, and Tsinghua University acts as a technical consultant to share its expertise in core technologies and China's food safety ecosystem. IBM and Tsinghua University plan to work with Wal-Mart and JD.com to develop and optimize blockchain technology and promote it to more suppliers and retailers joining the alliance.

For now, Jingdong has launched more than 100 brands to the chain, and more than 300 hot-selling products were linked to anti-counterfeiting traceability data blocks. Wal-Mart's tests show that by applying blockchain technology, the process of tracking a bag of mangoes from farm to store has been reduced from days to weeks to 2 seconds. And the time of food recall was significantly shortened, so the risk of food poisoning by consumers decreased significantly.

7.3 Secret of Chinese Success

China has proved itself as one of the leading countries in the application of blockchain, it is often said that it has taken over the second place in the world after the USA or even already replaced it. What is the reason for it? How could China achieve these results?

As early as December 2016, the State Council issued the "13th Five-Year National Informatization Plan", juxtaposing blockchain technology and new technologies such as the Internet of Things, cloud computing, big data, and artificial intelligence as a key engine in sustainable development and deepening structural reforms and promotion. On May 30, 2018, Xi Jinping during his speech at the 19th Academician Conference of the Chinese Academy of Sciences and the 14th Academician Conference of the Chinese Academy of Engineering affirmed the significance of the blockchain technology. "Since the 21st century, global science and technology innovation has entered an era of unprecedented activity. A new round of technological revolution and industrial transformation is reshaping the global innovation map and reshaping the global economic structure. A new generation of information technology, represented by artificial intelligence, quantum information, mobile communication, Internet of Things, and blockchain, accelerates breakthrough applications, and fosters new life sciences represented by synthetic biology, genetic editing, brain science, and regenerative medicine. The transformation, the advanced manufacturing technology that integrates robots, digital and new materials is accelerating the transformation of manufacturing to intelligent, service-oriented and green".

According to Reality Shares research, in August 2019, the number of patents related to blockchain applied by Chinese companies (1,338) is nearly three times more than US companies (442) and German companies (44) (Figure 7.1).

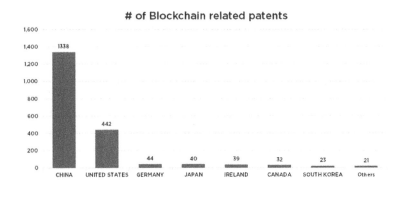

# of Blockchain related patents

Figure 7.1 Number of Blockchain related Patents by Country in 2019. (*Source*: China National Intellectual Property Administration.)

The number of blockchain patents owned by Chinese companies reached 68% of the global patent applications. The top three companies in the world – Alibaba (380), China United Network Communications (168), and Ping An Insurance (163) – are Chinese companies, and the fourth-ranked IBM (146) is based in the United States (Figure 7.2).

The Chinese government is also concerned about the functional aspects of the blockchain. Chinese government agencies have taken the lead in understanding block-chain projects at the public and corporate levels. China Information Industry Development Center regularly pub-lishes major public chain technology evaluation indexes and rankings such as Bitcoin, EOS, and Ethereum. The evaluation of these projects is based on their basic skills, applicability, and creativity.

In addition, starting in 2017, the government-approved China Electronics Standardization Institute (CESI) began

Rank	Company	Country	# of patents
1	Alibaba Group Holding Ltd	China	380
2	China United Network Communications	China	168
3	Ping An Insurance Group	China	163
4	International Business Machine	United States	146
5	Baidu Inc	China	141
6	ZhongAn Online P&C Insurance	China	126
7	Tencent Holdings Ltd	China	112
8	JD.com Inc	China	97
9	Mastercard Inc	United States	53
10	Bank of America Corp	United States	51

Source: Reality Shares, WIPO, China National Intellectual Property Administration. As of Aug. 22, 2019.

Figure 7.2 Top 10 Companies with the Most Number of Blockchain related Patents.

testing the functions of the standard blockchain system to verify the robustness of the top blockchain projects operating in China. The certification process is very rigorous and based on a wide range of guiding principles, taking into account the emerging nature of blockchain technology, which are very useful in unmanageable environments. Currently, only 30 projects have been certified. Certification is voluntary and not mandatory, but it is quite credible in the blockchain community.

Moreover, it looks like China is going to be the first country to apply digital currency (DCEP), based on blockchain. The People's Bank of China has been making research on it for 5–6 years and has already more than 40 patients.

The general idea is that they will adopt a two-layer operating system; that is, the People's Bank will first convert DCEP to the banks or other financial institutions, which will then be redeemed to the public. The significance of DCEP is that it is not a digitization of the existing currency, but an alternative to M0. It greatly reduces the dependency of the transaction to the account, which is conducive to the circulation and internationalization of the RMB. At the same time, DCEP can realize real-time collection of data such as currency creation, accounting, and flow, and provide a useful reference for the formulation of money and the creation and implementation of monetary policy.

So, highly supported and widely applied by the government, blockchain has already successfully landed in many industries and gained an obvious success in practical use in recent years in China.

Chapter 8

The Future of Cryptoeconomics

Steam engines provided power for human beings. Internet provided the computational platform for humans beings, and the blockchain will solve the credit problem for human beings.

The emergence of blockchain directly changes the production relations in the society, and we can expect that resources can be more fairly distributed. The fundamental for fairness in blockchain is that the formulation and implementation of rules are separated from the centralized organization and replaced by the consensus of peer-to-peer networks. Therefore, we need to look at the impacts of blockchain to the society more carefully again. In such circumstances, cryptoeconomics has emerged.

Trust has never been quantified because it is invisible and only exists in the perception between people. But the value of trust is so great. For example, the thief's damage to society is not only that it steals away the victim's wealth, but also causes unfairness. More importantly, the existence of thieves increases the cost of trust in the whole society.

What impact will the blockchain have on us after solving the basic trust problem? I think we can prospect from the following aspects: intermediator's services will slowly disappear, and it will allow the benefits to be distributed more quickly.

Intermediators exist because of the asymmetry of market information and the lack of trust between market counterparties. If you put this service on the chain, it will greatly improve the transaction efficiency between strangers, for example, rental market, second-hand trading market, and virtual goods market.

Because the trusted party is a smart contract rather than a person, the operating costs of the platform are very low, and the cost of the reduction can naturally benefit both buyers and sellers. Also, because the platform is trustworthy, and the right to confirm the goods is clear, it will certainly make it easier for people to make trading decisions, especially for relatively large transactions.

1. Sharing economy will further energize

   The most successful shared economic projects at this moment are Mobike and Didi Chuxing. But with the development of cryptoeconomics, I believe that such services will also be updated and iterated.

   Through the combination of blockchain and Internet of Things, future shared taxis might look like this:

I booked a taxi through my mobile phone. There is no driver in the taxi. After you pick up the phone, you have to enter the destination and calculate the price through the system, and after arrival to the destination, you pay and then the door opens. If you can't pay, then maybe you have to stay in the car. The same will be for the house. When the smart contract is implemented, if you don't pay the rent, then the lock becomes invalid.

In this way, both the user and the renter have fewer things to do. The most important is that there will be no financial differences, because they are all agreed, and no one can change the outcome.

2. Fans community management

In the future, society will generate more and more segmented communities, and these communities will all have their own unique values. For example: running, fitness, writing, music, movies, reading.... How can we make consensus in a shorter time? It is very likely that the community has its own token, has a smart contract that matches the community itself, and in the running community, records the distance and time of the campaign through special equipment, rewards for compliance, does not meet the standard penalty, or directly clears out. In fact, this will be a more reasonable and more harmonious society, because the rewards and punishments for you are not subjective individuals, but codes.

The ecological development of cryptoeconomics will greatly change the cooperation between people, the cooperation in the groups and between the groups, and even the cooperation between the state and the country. Because all of this is based on a new form of community, while building blockchain infrastructure we need to think more about the situation that we have never had before.

3. The application of cryptoeconomics

At present, there are many applications based and designed on cryptoeconomy. After solving the fundamental problem of the blockchain consensus, we can build various applications on the blockchain like Ethereum. Organizations and individuals can create their own. The value units used to motivate and punish, and design the conditional logic in different scenarios in the form of smart contract codes to achieve results that are currently unachievable.

For example, Signals, a trading strategy market, can achieve the goals through cryptoeconomics, and Signals uses its local token SGN to create a reward system. Any investor in the process of developing a trading strategy needs to refer to a variety of data, which often varies from person to person: some people may need the latest news of industry dynamics, while others prefer historical data.

Any investor can upload data that he or she considers important and unique to the Signals platform. Others need to pay a certain SGN token when using this data. If the user develops a successful trading strategy through the data, then initially the data uploader can achieve "fame and fortune", and if the data proves to be counterfeit or has no practical meaning, the uploader will be punished.

The above mechanism is also applicable for trading strategies designed by investors, which makes the decentralized trading strategy market possible.

Cryptoeconomics has also been used to design token sales or ICO. In some hot project crowdfunding, there are often cases when it is full of big customers, and retail investors are just "blinking" that means large households make a substantial increase in transaction fees, so that ordinary users do not have the opportunity to participate, and the concentration of tokens is higher, and it is far from the more away from the starting point of crowdfunding.

Therefore, in order to conduct more equitable token distribution, some projects use "Dutch auction" as a model for their token auctions. Dutch auctions refer to the auction bids declining from high to low until the first bidder strikes a deal when the price (at or above the reserve price). This has enabled the cryptoeconomy application to the field of auctions.

Whether it is the establishment of a low-level consensus agreement or the design of a better token sales mechanism, it can be seen as a cryptoeconomy. Building these applications requires an understanding of how incentives affect user's behavior, the design of economic mechanisms that reliably produce a result, and it is necessary to understand the functions and limitations of blockchain at the bottom layer that builds an application.

Of course, there are many blockchain applications that are not the product of cryptoeconomics. For example, Status and MetaMask, these application programs at the platforms and wallets that allow users to interact with the Ethereum blockchain. These mechanisms do not involve any other cryptoeconomics mechanism apart from those that are already part of bottom layer of blockchain.

Conclusion

Thinking about blockchain space from the cryptoeconomical point of view is very helpful. Once you have a certain understanding of cryptoeconomics, you can unlock many of the controversies and debates in our industry.

For example, a "licensing chain" that is with centralized management and does not use proof of effort has been controversial since it was first introduced. This area is often referred to as "distributed ledger technology", focusing on financial and business use cases. Many supporters of blockchain technology don't like this technology. These "license chains" are literally blockchains, but some of them are always weird. The "license chain" seems to reject something that everyone thinks is the focus of the blockchain: consensus can be reached without relying on a centrally trusted party or a traditional financial system.

The best way to distinguish them is to see if this blockchain is a product of cryptoeconomics. Just a simple distributed ledger, a blockchain that is based on cryptoeconomics design in order to reach consensus or adjust incentives, may be useful for some applications. But it is completely different from the one that is using cryptography and economic incentives to generate blockchains that have no previous consensus (such as Bitcoin and Ethereum). These are two different technologies, and the best way to distinguish them is to see if they are the product of cryptoeconomics.

Also, we should expect that there will be cryptoeconomics consensus agreements that do not depend on "blocks" and "chains" in the future. Obviously, this technique has something in common with blockchain technology, but it is not correct to call them blockchains. We need to look at whether such an agreement is a product of cryptoeconomics, not whether it is a blockchain.

ICO focuses on this distinction, but there are few clear explanations. One of the strongest manifestations of the value of a token is that many people independently realize = whether it constitutes an integral part of the application to which it is connected. To say it more clearly: is the token a necessary part of the cryptoeconomics mechanism in application program? That's the reason why understanding the mechanism design in the ICO project is crucial for determining the utility and value of the token.

In the past few years, we have been thinking about this new field from the perspective of only one application (bitcoin), and we have shifted to the perspective of the bottom layer technology (blockchain). We now need to take a step back and look at this type of solution in a unified way, that is, cryptoeconomics.

Index